By Emily Churchill Wood

© 2015 by Emily Churchill Wood

Published by
Joe Harwell Publishing
9023 E. 46th St. #54213
Tulsa, OK 74155-0213
joeharwell54@gmail.com

Cover Designer: Melissa A. Robitille
robitille@gmail.com

ISBN-10: 1523730021
ISBN-13: 978-1523730025

Find retail locations on the Facebook page
http://on.fb.me/1ogMOqA

This is my version and my memory of life with Phil. I accept that others may have a different perception of the story of our life. We all see life differently as it happens, but for me, it truly was magic.

To Dr. John Hubner
with gratitude
and appreciation.
Emily Wood

This book is dedicated with love and best wishes to our beloved children, Martha, Arthur, Benjamin and Warren. All profits from this book will be donated to the Juvenile Diabetes Research Foundation in hope that a cure is found.

Table of contents

Chapters   Page

Introduction

This book is my story of the evolution of my seventy-one years of shared love with Phil Wood, a sublime partnership. A backward look tells me that constantly learning to communicate honestly and completely was the key. World War II, the corporate prosperity of the fifties, the Cold War, the Civil Rights movement, man on the moon, environmental threats, the Vietnam War, assassinations, Watergate, computerization, Gulf and Iraq Wars, and the election of our first black president, Barack Obama, were some of the events providing the background for our ever deepening relationship and love. These events impacted us and our children even more. Our solid and stable childhoods allowed us the luxury of communication, love, adventure and excitement. Both of us were winners in a win/win relationship.

Writing this story has been a revelation. I started out to write a fact filled memoir. Soon I found I was writing a love story as tears rolled down my cheeks when I thought of the beautiful experiences we shared - the moon, sunsets, the birth of our children, the smiles, the reunions after separations, adventures, travels and much, much more. We were soulmates, lovers, friends, partners and co-parents.

Writing this story revealed that communication was the key to growing together. Sharing thoughts openly and honestly was not easy. Truly listening to a partner was not easy. Communicating included verbal communication, body language, doing and actions, tokens and gifts, touch, clothes, habits like being on time, and more. Being conscious of constant communication was a growth experience.

Writing this story revealed how we were children of our times. We were able to adapt to the separation of World War II, the expectations of corporate America, changes in the role of women, changes in careers, being parents, grandparents, and great grandparents. Change was always welcome. We were proud members of the greatest generation.

Writing this book gave me appreciation for our solid and stable childhoods. Even though we were raised during the Depression, our fathers worked steadily. Phil's father was a researcher at Bell Labs and my father was an advertising executive in NYC. Both were self-made men and very grateful for their middle class prosperity. Our mothers were both graduates of the elite Seven Sister Colleges, lived earlier in Greenwich Village, NYC, and shared an appreciation for art and classical music. Both sets of parents had high expectations and standards for their children. We were blessed.

Writing this memoir made me realize that life for our children was not as easy or simple for them as it was for us. We were not always sensitive to the huge impact that corporate moving, with its change of schools and loss of friends could have. We were not always conscious of how our own romantic fascination with each other and extensive adult social life could impact our children. We veered from the more rigid expectation and rules of our parents to the child raising philosophy of Dr. Spock. We, however, did always read bedtime stories, cuddle in bed, picnic, swim, go to museums, eat regular dinners with discussion, camp, attend all school events and games, hike, skate, sled, celebrate holidays with gusto, bake cookies, dye Easter eggs, etc.. We enjoyed parenting. Our four children have all turned into the most caring, loving people imaginable. They care deeply about other people and the world. We only wished we could have guaranteed them a life as pain free as we lived together.

Telling this story has been immensely helpful to me as I mix gratitude with grief.

Phil and I, covered with therapeutic mud, are shown at the Dead Sea, Israel, in 1995. This was one of many exciting adventures on trips sponsored by Tulsa Sister Cities and Tulsa Global Alliance.

Chapter 1. Death-2013
Age 88

Philip Warren Wood, 88, died at St. John's Hospital, Tulsa, Oklahoma at 4:48 pm on November 20, 2013, after five days of hospice care, from internal bleeding, a complication of Non-Hodgkin's Lymphoma. His last words were "You have been fabulous. I tried but now I want to die. I love you."

He was in pain. Drugs eased him into a deep sleep for five days and only once more did he try to talk, but even though heartfelt, it was not understandable. Verbal communication was over, but his demeanor demonstrated profound acceptance and calm. The entire time as he slumbered looking so very handsome and contented, I felt he was listening when his family told him they loved him. He was listening when our Unitarian minister, Marlin Lavanhar, told him he could transition with the knowledge of having done a great job of living and taking care of me.

Choir music and staff from All Souls Church, beautiful yellow roses, fall foliage, his family and friends eased his leaving until he easily took his last breath. The choir communicated love beyond belief. His children stroked his brow.

Family tears from children and grandchildren communicated care and loss. The yellow roses from the church communicated joy and beauty. I felt that Phil was absorbing the positive vibes and giving them back until he had no pulse, and our dear Dr. John Hubner confirmed death to a loving family. So many people die many times before they really die. Phil only died once after a life very well lived.

The twenty-three days before Phil's death were the most precious times of togetherness as I slept in his hospital room and only left for a very quick hour to get clean clothes or eat a bite in the cafeteria. In spite of countless transfusions, internal bleeding, procedures, sporadic pain and even operations, it was a time of optimistic smiles. I was always amazed at how he could emerge on a gurney from an operating room with the hospital hat on his head and a smile on his face and greet me with a "Hello, dearie". I would say, "You are the handsomest person ever wheeled through the hospital halls."

He did crossword puzzles and word searches continuously to the last day and enjoyed having grandchildren do homework in his room. He often looked over and waved during the night to see if I was on the pullout couch, and I would wave back. He would give a meaningful look. We felt that he would get better, so it was not a time of worry and distress but of cherishing being together. My laptop computer kept me in constant communication with far flung family. Tulsa family visited often. Our daughter from New Jersey was there for the last five day vigil to join Tulsa kin. Seventy one years of heartfelt communication which started with a glance and eyes locking across a crowded colonial style church in Summit, New Jersey continue after Phil's death in Tulsa, Oklahoma. I write him letters communicating remembrance and gratitude. I talk to him when I listen to beautiful music or see an exquisite flower.

Looking back, we were incredibly privileged to have had fathers who worked throughout the Great Depression, nurturing mothers and grandparents, great regular healthy family meals, books, lessons, nice homes, vacations, a war that united the country, veterans benefits galore including the G-I bill, a growing postwar economy where jobs with benefits were plentiful. All of this left us free to enjoy a fabulous love, four wonderful children, great careers, arts enrichment, community service, adventure, and unbounded fun with friends. These circumstances enabled us to be free to communicate fully and fearlessly.

We were blessed and we both knew it. I do not think that we ever succeeded in fully walking in the shoes of those who suffered from segregation and discrimination, the effects of the Vietnam War, poverty and a host of other ills. However, we were sympathetic and supportive although not always as active and empathetic as we could have been.

Our hospital goodbyes were beautiful as was the Memorial Service at All Souls. Family love, friends, food and flowers were omnipresent. Then on Thanksgiving Day, my first experience of numbing, debilitating, incapacitating grief kept me in a fetal position in bed dimly aware of the noises and smell of the preparation and consumption of a gourmet turkey dinner by seventeen children and grandchildren with spouses and girlfriends. Tears flowed that had been largely absent in the hospital and the following days of friends' visits and preparations. Never had I felt such a void and sadness. It was my first experience with real grief.

The next day I woke with flashes of gratitude which became part of the mourning. The gratitude was for the many years of unbelievable love, for my wonderful children, two of whom were here from New York and for the many expressions of caring from friends and colleagues. I realized that I must try. Phil tried. So I decided to try. I chose life and a brand of grief that was laced with a huge component of gratitude and action.

Chapter 2. Glances, Smiles, First Letters, Kisses

1941 - 1943 Ages 16 - 18

Glances exchanged with Phil at the Community Unitarian Church in suburban Summit, NJ, during the electrifying sermons of soon to be famous Washington D.C. minister, A. Powell Davies are my first recollection of a strong and forever attraction between us. We were both sixteen-year-old seniors during this autumn of 1941, learning of Hitler's fatal movements through newsreels, newspapers and Dr. Davies' passionate sermons. The bombing of Pearl Harbor on December 7, 1941, brought the U.S. into the war. As we glanced at each other with admiration, impending war intensified our feelings.

Phil, called Phippy in 1941, attended this church with his mother, Sally Wood, from nearby Chatham. Emily accompanied her fellow, uniformed, makeup–free boarders from Kent Place School for Girls. Her mother, Ruth Pierson Churchill, had long been an active trustee and

Sunday school teacher, having traded a strong and respected Methodist family heritage for the freedom from creed of the Summit church.

The glances at church continued throughout our senior years (Phil at Chatham High). When I, class president, led my class down a beautiful grassy slope at graduation, Phil was at the bottom beaming at me. A picture of his handsome, welcoming smiling face is still crystal clear in my mind. He gave me the first of his many stellar smiles of approval, which were to nurture and thrill me for seventy-two years until his last smile for me at St. John's Hospital in Tulsa, Oklahoma. His smiles and glances lasted a lifetime. I was the co-winner of the Citizenship Cup recognizing my high school years as a rule follower, rule enforcer, study hall monitor, leader etc., but pleasure from that honor was eclipsed by seeing him.

War time brought me a summer job doing piece work in a Rhode Island zipper factory producing assembly line olive drab fasteners for military gear. Labor was needed in factories to replace the men already at war and to meet the demand for vast amounts of equipment. My eyes were opened when I realized my much faster fellow worker was supporting three children on the eighteen dollars we were paid each week. Men were going to war and were scarce in the workplace. This job brought me my first Social Security card, a recent phenomenon of President Franklin

Delano Roosevelt's administration. I am enjoying the Social Security perk today even though it was opposed by my Republican father in 1935.

I lived with two Kent Place friends in a beautiful home near Narragansett Bay. We rode our bikes to our 3-11 pm shift with lots of whistling and cat calls from young males on the streets of Providence. We kept our eyes down and rode fast. Gasoline was rationed and bikes were the transportation mode.

Meanwhile, Phil had matriculated at Princeton following his father, 1915, and his brother, Darwin, 1942. Ernest Wood, a distinguished researcher at Bell Labs, held both a B.S. and a Master's degree in physics from Princeton. A farm boy from Pennsylvania, he taught rural school until arriving at Princeton with a sack of potatoes and a great will to succeed. He worked his way completely through college by working in and managing the dining halls.

Ernest's love for Princeton was zealous and unbounded in gratitude for a transformed life. Ernest served, with honor and pride in France as Captain during World War I. He married Sally, a daughter of the Presbyterian minister who was a scholarly teacher of Greek and Latin. Ernest had extremely high standards for himself and his family as they moved with upward mobility through the 1920s and the Great Depression.

Phil and his fellow classmates had World War II on their minds when they arrived for the summer of 1942 at the all men's college. They knew that when they turned eighteen, they would be off to military service. Eat drink and be merry was their prevailing philosophy. The end of the summer brought a couple of casual dates with Phil in Chatham, and then he was off back to Princeton and I to Smith College by train to start my freshman year.

I was thrilled to receive an invitation to a football weekend in Princeton from Phippy, a family nickname. This was a dream come true after my sequestered girls' school life. The three part train ride brought me to Princeton junction where he awaited with his classic welcoming smile. I checked into the girls' boarding house and after dinner on Nassau Street we walked and walked. Under the beautiful gothic tower of the Graduate School with a full moon we kissed for the first time. I remember that star struck magic. I do not remember who played Princeton the next day. Phil came to the Charity Ball at Smith that 1942 December, bringing several Princeton friends for my Smith friends.

One subsequent blind date with a slobbery kiss at an Amherst fraternity party convinced me that I never, ever wanted to kiss anyone but Phil.

Letters from Phil's 1943 winter semester talk about his
friends, Princeton social activities and his growing love but
little about his studies or the war. In January, he wrote that
he and Al Taylor, his roommate acquired "a rams head
with a pipe in its mouth" which had been left by a
"previous graduate" to cover a bare wall in their spacious
suite of rooms. He goes on to say, "You guessed it. If we
did that, when did we study? Oh well there is always
tomorrow. It would be awfully nice to grow sleepy with
you playing Pomp and Circumstance or reading Thurber or
Ogden Nash with you. I won't contrast growing sleepy
with you with a German book because there is no
comparison. All the same I wish I could be with you."

On Jan 21, 1943, he wrote, "Life isn't so bad after all. I just
finished my last exam. I hardly know how to treat my time.
It is like a convict getting out of prison. Anyway, I send
you all my love. Speaking of which, have you noticed the
moon lately? The nights have been clear and cold and the
moon has been positively beautiful. (Tear marks) Please
pardon the sentimental tone of that."

The moon remained a sentimental symbol for us always.
Letters talked of going to all the hockey games with Al
Taylor and cheering wildly for Princeton. Letters also tell
of fun with future brother- in- law Chuck Drake and the
ultimate prank of stealing the clapper from the bell in the

tower of Nassau Hall with Al, Chuck and friend Jim Lipscomb.

His longest letter started, "Emmy Darling" and then detailed the three borrowed ladder ascensions of Nassau Hall spanning two nights with a final successful removal of the clapper. He wrote at 3:15 a.m. on the night of March 17, 1943, "I went and got Chuck ...together we got Jim. Jim found us a couple of high grade wrenches and the result is that the 30 or 40 pound clapper is now under my bed ...I thought that you should know what wonderful people Chuck, Al, Jim and I are … All My Love, Phippy." Stealing the clapper was an accepted prank in those days at Princeton. The clapper was returned to Princeton many, many years later by Liz Drake when her son Chuck was becoming a noted geophysicist and professor at Dartmouth.

Letters were the major form of communication for Phil and me. The telephone was too expensive and saved for only very important and unusual situations. My letters from Smith to him got lost, but I am sure that I kept him informed of my studies in art history, psychology, English, required Freshman Hygiene, European History and trouble with Spanish pronunciation and wonderful new friends.

I am sure I also wrote to thank him profusely for a fabulous time when we met in NYC for a chaste weekend with Chuck Drake and his date. We stayed on segregated and chaperoned dormitory floors at the Biltmore Hotel after a romantic meeting under the clock. Entertainment was all free - Central Park Zoo, Natural History Museum, Staten Island ferry and walking, walking, walking. Meals were at the automat. It was a glorious time of discovering a life-long mutual enjoyment of museums, zoos and ferry boats.

A last letter from Princeton announced he would be called up for service at a date still unknown. He talked about how very much he would miss me, but said we were too young to marry. He also said he did not want me to be subjected to the life of a soldier's wife. The prankster who stole the clapper and teased my Smith friends with practical jokes showed great maturity when making major life decisions. This would be mantra always - humor, fun and games galore within a well-examined and well-planned life.

Our freshman year was a valuable time of learning to communicate by speaking and writing as well as holding hands, kissing and hugging. It was a good beginning for two people who had recently turned eighteen. World War II was a reality. Three English children, escaping the London blitz, had been living with Phil's parents for three years. I had two classmates from England who were escaping Hitler's bombs at Kent Place. Our parents had Victory Gardens. My Mother served on the Rationing

Board and biked everywhere. Everyone was solidly behind
the war and extremely patriotic. Now, Phippy was about to
go.

Autumn 1943, Phil and I, third and fourth from left, on
date at Smith College for Charity Ball. We were seventeen
year old college freshmen. Phil would return with me
regularly until my 60th reunion in 2006.

Emily,

I stumbled upon this picture today – reminding me of our all abiding love!

Love, Phil

We experienced our first kiss standing by the tower of the Princeton Graduate Tower on a beautiful moonlit October night in 1943. Our last return to this site was in 2006 at Phil's 60th reunion. He wrote the note during the 1990s. This picture of the tower still brings tears to my eyes.

L to R, Best friend and future brother-in-law, Chuck Drake, Jim Lipscomb, roommate Al Taylor and Phil proudly display the clapper taken from Princeton bell tower during a dark night while avoiding the surveillance of the proctors. Stealing the clapper was a venerable Princeton tradition at that time.

PRINCETON UNIVERSITY LIBRARY
PRINCETON, NEW JERSEY

· 4 December 1956

Dear Mr. Wood:

On behalf of the Trustees of Princeton University, I have the

honor to acknowledge the receipt of

            Nassau Hall bell clapper
(The gift of you and Mr. Charles L. Drake '45).

which you have presented to the Library of the University, and I beg you

to accept their sincere thanks for the gift.

                              I am

                         Yours sincerely,

                         William S. Dix

                              Librarian

Mr. Philip W. Wood
477 West Napier
Benton Harbor
Michigan

Chapter 3. World War Two

1943 - 1946 Ages 18 - 21

Private Phil arrived at Camp Hale, Colorado via troop train after basic training at Fort Dix, New Jersey as a member of the 86th Infantry 10th Mountain Division, popularly known as the ski troops. Camp Hale was created in the majestic Rocky Mountains west of Leadville. Some of the men were world famous skiers who in the post bellum era created the famous Vail ski resort. Many were recruits from Ivy League colleges. Others were muleskinners to care for the many mules needed to move supplies and gear through high altitude paths.

On June 7, 1943, his letter read, "My Darling, I'm sitting on top of the world. This is the first time I've really felt chipper since I have been in the army. You can ask the boys. This the first time I've sung since I have been here. And you can claim the credit. You sent me a letter and I received it this evening. If you think this is fantastic, you do not know what the army is …

I'm becoming quite a philosopher. I can now grovel in the dirt… and still be in an ivory tower. Isn't that disgusting? I'm really not bad though. I'm sociable and get along well with the boys. There is an Alaskan in the bunk below mine and a boxer from Manchester, New Hampshire next to me.

It's awfully interesting to see the different types of men around here….

Today, we had rifle marksmanship… Both the Sergeant and the Lieutenant came up to me and complimented me… I was the best in the company. That is the first good thing that has actually happened to me. Not that I'm always messing things up, but that is the first time I have had a time to shine. I guess my hunting at Aunt Helen's and Wyalusing is paying off. Enough of this bragging but I have to tell someone…

Thanks again for sending me the wonderful letter. It was a great tonic…"

Sharing our triumphs was a lifelong joyous habit that started early and spontaneously. A joy shared is a joy doubled just as a sorrow shared is a sorrow halved. He said, "I have to tell someone…" I loved to be that someone. I loved being the someone who could send a letter which could be a great tonic. I also loved having someone in whom to confide every triumph and worry. I was learning to listen, the greatest of all communication skills.

At Camp Hale besides shooting, Phil learned skiing for miles with a heavy backpack, mountain climbing, rappelling down cliffs, digging sleeping holes in the snow, performing vigorous chores at high altitudes and other skills a soldier would need in mountainous combat. Letters described the beauty and majesty of the Rockies and the enjoyment of discovering Denver on pass with fellow soldier Herb Lauterwasser, a classmate from Chatham High, also in serving in the 10th Mountain Division. Phil also later told of having to dig a very large hole for the Sergeant because of a minor rule infraction and questioning of authority. He later recalled he did it with good humor whistling all the way. We later met the noncom at a reunion in Texas. We speculated that his discipline may have helped Phil rise through corporate ranks and have the temperament to be a judicious auditor in later years.

No existing letter documents why Phil was sent to the University of Nebraska in Lincoln to study engineering in December, 1943, but he wrote his most uncharacteristically negative letters ever from there. At the time, his dream was to become an MD – not an engineer.

He wrote, "Emmy darling, The U.S. Army has just made one of its worst mistakes in history. I am now an engineer. This training will no doubt be good for my character and revive my mind, but it's a useless waste of time because I am going to be a sawbones anyway. The thing that really bothers me is how many years will it be before I can get married. I am all confused. The only thing that I am not confused about is that I love you as much as ever."

Phil turned nineteen while in Nebraska and continued to talk about the long wait it would be until we got married, because medical school was on his mind. In January 1944, he wrote, "I am praying to get a furlough so that I can come home and hold you in my arms again."

He was sent back to Camp Hale for winter maneuvers as an infantryman in the snow at temperatures of thirty-five below. Then in the spring the whole 10th Mountain Division, including thousands of mules, moved to Camp Swift, Texas for flatland training in preparation for Italian combat.

On July 19, 1944 from Camp Swift Texas, he wrote, "My Darling, Yes, I am still here. The training has become more strenuous during the past week. Yesterday, we got up bright and early at 4:00 and didn't go to bed until 3:00 this morning. However, we were allowed to sleep until 7:00 - big deal! Included in that day was an infiltration course. It isn't bad crawling under machine gun fire at night, but the sand was very annoying. Everything without exception was filled with sand. I was in the pits holding targets to fire at this week …

I still hope for a furlough sometime. Emmy, you've no idea how well I feel that you want to get engaged. I love you so much I want everyone to know. I have been thinking about you more and more as the training gets tougher, darling. I guess I just like to think about the most pleasant thing that I know as an escape.

I got into a very interesting discussion with some good lads the other day. It started out on the subject of whether the South could be brought to the economic level of the North. Anyhoo - it came around to my pet theory that education and opportunity for education should be offered as a reward for work rather than capital. It may sound like Lenin but I like it… One of the lads is the husband of my sister's roommate in college and is also a Harvard law grad. The other two were an architect from Seattle and Sonja Henie's skating partner. What a group! It's a good thing that they were talking about something which I have thought about. I shall always be as infatuated as when I am saturated, darling. Your adoring suitor, Phippy."

Phil always made friends ready for a "bull session" wherever he was. In later civilian life, the bull sessions took the form of lively dinner table conversations with friends or family.

Phil did get a furlough in August of 1944 and we were formally and joyously engaged at a family party. We went to New York City to get my engagement ring. I fainted dead away on the floor when it was put on my finger. What emotion! What drama! What romance! All four parents were absolutely delighted and thrilled. My parents were overjoyed that Phil was light-hearted, handsome, smiling and knew how to enjoy life. His parents were delighted that he was getting a hard working student who was on the serious side.

Phil was a prolific letter writer that fall from Camp Swift. He was diagnosed with flat feet during a routine check and moved out of the infantry into the Medical Corps where he became a mail clerk. At first he missed the infantry. He took up pencil drawing and found it very relaxing. He went to San Antonio and Austin on passes.

Tragedy struck in November. Phil's wonderful mother, Sally, died of a cerebral hemorrhage at age 53. The Red Cross flew Phil home on his first airplane flight. I took the train home from Smith and fell into my handsome soldier's arms at Grand Central Station. After the New Jersey funeral, we drove with father Ernest and brother Dar on a cold, dark, bleak dismal day for the burial in Wyalusing, PA, at the cemetery next to Sally's childhood home, Merryall Manse. Phil had spent much childhood time there.

This was my first visit of many. Seventy years later we left some of Phil's ashes there on a beautiful, sunny 4th of July, 2014, with a large crowd of family at the informal loving service. He is remembered in the cemetery with a bronze plaque mounted on granite which says Philip Warren Wood, United States Army.

Mother Sally Cook was born at the manse. She and her third child, Phippy, always shared a special loving bond. In the short time between our engagement and her death, she wrote me several wonderful letters about how happy she was about us. She said, "we were just right" for each other. She was correct. We were just right for each other.

Phil spent the rest of his bereavement furlough at Smith College. I remember as a special privilege my housemother let us sit in the living room outside of her bedroom from 10:15 when dorm doors were locked until midnight!!! - a huge concession. Times have changed since then.

In the plane on the way back to Camp Swift, Phil wrote, "My dearest darling …You can probably guess what a magnificent time I had with you, Best Beloved, but I will tell you anyway. I had a magnificent time. I hope that doesn't sound badly considering the reason I was home, but I know that is the way mother would want it. It would be very wrong to say that I wasn't sad on this furlough considering the reason that I was home but long faces never helped anybody at all. I am glad that I appreciated mother and realized what she has given me. If I had not realized it before I know it would dawn on me now and it would have made things even tougher for me… I just looked out the window and we've climbed above the clouds. It is most 'scruciating' beautiful out. The moon is shining on the wing and we're just skimming along a sea of white fluff." Phil continued to love to look at clouds and share his thoughts about them verbally throughout his life. When I look at clouds today, I often tear up thinking about him.

For Christmas 1944, he gave me a Savings Bond with a letter explaining that this was the beginning of a lifetime of saving together. Both of us considered this a very romantic gift as well as a realistic commitment to life as a couple. Our life long team philosophy of money management was agreed upon, facilitating stress free long term open financial communication and planning for the next 69 years. This was a huge statement of shared values. I look back on this bond purchase as being the foundation of my great financial security as a widow today.

Letters stopped as the 10th Mountain Division, 12,200 strong shipped out across the Atlantic to Italy landing in January of 1945. Phil later recounted that he was one of the very few who was not seasick enabling him to smoke cigars on deck and consume large quantities of the rations that others did not want before landing in Leghorn, Italy. The objective of the 10th Mountain Division was to secure the Po Valley. Wresting the rugged hills and mountains from the Germans was very costly in terms of casualties. The division was in combat for 114 days with 975 killed and 3,871 wounded. The orders were to capture Mt. Belvedere. The taking of Route 64 enabled crossing the Po River and proceeding north to occupy the village of Malcesine on the shores of Lake Garda.

From Malcesine he wrote, "It is beautiful country, eh? You would never know that here had been a war here." The war in Italy ended on May 2, 1945. As the division rolled north, they were welcomed by throngs of happy Italians rejoicing with cheers and bottles of wine for the American liberators. One bystander gifted Phil with his gun. Phil's job as a mail clerk for the 10th Medical Battalion entailed often driving a truck many miles a day, often through mountain passes to pick up the precious mail and take it back to the men in the field in the Po Valley campaign. Mail was a precious morale builder.

Phil and good friend, Jim Lill, future professor at the University of Oregon, used free evenings in 1944 to produce a two page newspaper, "The Boar's Nest" full of satire, comments and humor. The masthead stated that it was published at Censored Italy, whenever the mood strikes the Editors. I was listed as a foreign correspondent. "The idea for the paper materialized in a fashion that no one can actually trace. Perhaps it is best to say that it was born in an interesting bull session, which in turn was started by some even more interesting Italian cognac."

Between May and July, 1945, when the division sailed to the USA to be deployed to the Pacific, Phil had a fantastic experience that he treasured for the rest of his life. Strictly on the basis of an IQ test (he had the highest in his battalion), he was sent to Florence to help unpack the incredible art treasures that had been packed away during the war for safety. This was an unbelievable opportunity being near the work of the masters and working on a project led by the great art historian DeWald. He walked the streets of Florence and visited nearby Venice during what was the experience of a lifetime while the 10th division waited in Yugoslavia.

In July 1945, the division sailed home with the expectation of fighting Japan. Phil came home on furlough. We hitchhiked (war time custom because there was gas rationing) to visit my parents at a summer resort in the Pocono Mountains. When we arrived at a juncture of highways in Harrisburg, PA, bells started ringing, sirens went off. Japan had surrendered. We were hugging, kissing, shouting, and dancing in the streets with everyone from the stopped cars. It was an unbelievable moment of shared joy as we realized the war was over and Phil would not be deployed again. With all the motorists at that roundabout, we were together celebrating our love in great, great excitement. Only later, did we learn about the Atomic Bomb. It was an incredibly well-kept secret. In 1982, when we visited Nagasaki as tourists we comprehended the destruction and suffering caused in Japan by the bomb as we saw charred bones and bodies.

Phil finished his army experience at Letterman General Hospital as an ombudsman in beautiful San Francisco tracking down medals and paperwork for wounded soldiers. An Italian-American family adopted him for Thanksgiving and Christmas. He loved exploring the city. Most of all we loved setting our wedding date. He was discharged in spring of 1946. I continued at Smith taking honors and writing a thesis on the Russo-Finnish War and chairing the first Honor Board in the history of the college as well as serving on the student council. Working on farms with a Smith contingent had been my wartime service.

After discharge and return to Princeton, Phil visited Smith on a few weekends endearing himself to my friends. My friends became his friends and were OUR friends for life. Of course at graduation, the first thing I noticed was his big smile at me when I received my cum laude diploma. He looked so handsome in his seersucker suit and white bucks. The commencement address that year focused on how graduates could be helpmates as wives and mothers as very educated women with advice to join the League of Women voters. I was thrilled that one week after my graduation, wife I would become. Our anticipation and joy were boundless.

Phil's mother had this beloved picture taken during a short furlough after basic training at Fort Dix, NJ. It sat on my dresser at Smith College. He was eighteen. It sits on my bedside table today.

Phil, 1943, at Camp Hale was taught rock climbing skills and other mountain skills. Army Camp Hale, in the background, was created quickly to house the 10th Mt. Division.

Phil is in right lower corner taking a break on maneuvers at Camp Hale.

Phil and I, August, 1944, at small engagement party. We both were thrilled to make our love and commitment known to the world.

Engagement with Phil's family, August, 1944. L to R, Brother Darwin, Emily, Phil, Mother Sally and Father Ernest. Sadly, Phil's Mother Sally died of a cerebral hemorrhage three months later.

World War II, Emily on left picking tomatoes on Massachusetts farm with Smith College friends. A favorite activity was taking produce to Boston Market at night. We lived together dormitory style.

During World War II, I cherished the letters from Phil. I
am shown here reading during a break at Veg Acre Farms.
The huge broccoli farm was maintained by a cadre of
Smith students and a few male conscientious objectors.

World War II, on furlough at Smith College. I was all dressed up and not wearing my usual blue jeans.

We were with Marilyn Kieckhefer from Milwaukee, my
four year roommate on the steps of Talbot House while
Phil was on furlough. Phil and I visited Marilyn and her
husband, Tom, in Milwaukee many times during the next
fifty years.

Phil is shown on furlough at Smith College with his father's borrowed car.

Phil's job in Italy was to process and transport mail from his battalion. He drove many miles over and between mountains. Notice vehicles in background.

Phil, in middle, acted as an ombudsman for wounded soldiers at Letterman Military Hospital in the Presidio in San Francisco.

EMILY AND PHIL VISITED MALCESINA, ITALY IN JUNE 2001

THIS IS THE SPOT WHERE PHIL WAS SERVING WITH THE 10TH MT. DIV. ON THE DAY WWII ENDED IN EUROPE.

Italy 2001. Emily and Phil at the site where Phil was when victory in Europe occurred in 1945.

Chapter 4. Wedding and Vows

June 22, 1946 - Age 21

All organizations, partnerships, governments, institutions and marriages must have a core communication of values and goals to survive and grow. For the United States, it is the Constitution. For our marriage, our pledge, our agreement, our promise came from our wedding vows taken at the simple white colonial Unitarian church in Summit, New Jersey in a simple ceremony with light shining through clear windows, with guests sitting on caned chairs.

The ceremony was followed by an elegant reception at the Morris County Country Club, which was meticulously planned by my mother, Ruth Churchill and a very competent wedding planner. Every detail was perfect and beautiful from my long tulle veil and Phil's immaculate tail coat for the after five wedding to the sumptuous food, music and two hundred guests. My dear Daddy paid for it.

The party reflected the sociability, good taste and joy of my parents. Phil and I enjoyed every moment of the elegant soiree and were happy to leave the vast amount of planning to my mother. Phil and I were completely into the anticipation of marrying at last after a four year wait. Phil was grinning from ear to ear, and I could only think of him.

Looking back our vows at the church constituted the pact that made all other communication and actions possible for sixty-seven years and five months. We had a core set of precepts for all of our decisions. I do not think we ever wavered from these for a moment through life's challenges - careers, economic considerations, many moves, raising children and grandchildren. The wedding vows were our Constitution.

We promised to love and to cherish for richer or poorer, to have and to hold, forsaking all others in sickness and health until death do us part. Death did part us on November 20, 2013, with the vows intact. I did not promise to obey, an idea counter to both our beliefs.

In sickness and health - As I stayed with him day and night in the hospital during his last twenty-three days on earth, I reflected on how he stood by me as nurse, psychologist, lover, and husband during my nose surgery to fix a neglected basal cell in 1997. A flap of skin taken from my forehead and behind my ears turned me into a temporary monster. He took me home from the procedure and immediately set up a post-op tray with sterile gloves, antiseptic and dressings to process the wound. He followed the surgeon's precise instructions to the tee. Phil's demeanor was calm and efficient and inspired my complete confidence. He covered the mirrors in the house to hide the horrible vision. He assured me that he did not love my nose, he loved me. He brought in food that we ate after our usual cocktail and made it a party for two. He balanced auditing at the city with visits home for care, comfort and food. In other words, he kept his cool all the time.

He went to Saks Fifth Avenue and bought me the most beautiful black hat and attached an opaque veil, which I could see through but which shielded the public from a view of my grotesque nasal organ. The hat attested to his always impeccable taste when he bought me clothes. Soon we were out and about in the world wearing my hat. The doctor and nurses were amazed by the clean healing of the wound and pronounced his nursing skills amazing. The stitches came out. The flap was gone. My nose was an unfamiliar protuberance. Life resumed with campaigns, elections, parties, teaching, traveling, and loving more and more deeply and soulfully.

For richer, for poorer - strangely, this vow demanded the most adjustment. After ten or so years of corporate striving, saving, moving with the eye on tomorrow, Phil became a very young regional manager with a very large office on Michigan Avenue in Chicago, with office staff as well as teams of technical representatives on the road. He also had a generous expense account paying for the best dinners and hotels. He enjoyed being boss. My life had not changed much. His raises helped but did not change my life. I had a period of depression, fatigue and anxiety. A psychologist in three sessions prescribed more fun together, which was an instant cure, as we used the new found money for dance and bridge lessons. The dancing was a lifelong blessing and pleasure for more than sixty-five years, culminating at grandson Nick's wedding. The vows, our Constitution, always allowed us to make our decisions putting our relationship first without guilt. It became easy to give up an invitation for one of us to an event with a friend or relative, whether it was a cruise or an international vacation (this was not always true when business was involved).

We both believed fiercely in guidelines and plans especially in the United States Constitution. Phil always carried a copy of it in his pocket and took seriously upholding it as auditor. I delighted in the teacher institutes in Philadelphia, where the Constitution was born. Phil joined me there. Studying the Constitution together brought us together in unison in our political beliefs as we voted, hoping the outcomes would help the many enjoy the healthcare insurance that we the privileged enjoyed. We attended Democratic lunches together and enjoyed the help and support of Tulsa's labor unions. We were grateful to FDR for our Social Security and the G.I. Bill, which left us debt free after a first class education.

We believed in the U.S. Constitution, the big plan for our government. We believed in our wedding vows, the overall plan for our marriage. Both were to form a "more perfect union" and both could last through changing times.

Phil and I in NYC in June, 1946, at a beautiful pre-wedding party at the St. Regis Hotel given by Emily's Uncle Ed and Aunt Bitsy Churchill.

Wedding reception. L to R, Phil's father, Ernest, Phil, Emily, Emily's mother, Ruth, and father, Arthur. My parents planned and gave us a beautiful, fun wedding.

We sang at the wedding reception. It was a joyous occasion.

Smiles express joy as Phil and Emily left the wedding reception for their honeymoon in the Adirondacks. They were husband and wife.

After nose surgery, at Mother Ruth's in NJ in 1997. Phil reassured me he did not marry my nose. He kept his wedding vows.

Chapter 5. The Marriage Bed
1946 - 2013

Sex is all about communication. Sex grew from something we longed for and yearned for during the war years to a complete soulful experience in our eighties transcending all boundaries separating our beings. Sex grew from doing what comes naturally to a truly sublime physical spiritual experience. It began on our wedding night in 1946 and was ended by a drug used to treat lymphoma in March, 2013. Cuddles, illness, gratitude, handholding and love were the aftermath until death parted us nine months later. It was a wonderful run spanning a time of changing sexual mores in the country. We never wanted a king size bed. It was too big for the cuddles that warmed aching muscles, soothed racing brains, and brought peaceful relaxation for sixty-six plus years.

World War II was raging. Phil was in the army. The army recognized the great libido of young virile men. Venereal diseases had horrible consequences that could not be treated because penicillin was not yet available except in the very limited supplies for battlefield use. Young soldiers were required to view graphic and sobering films showing the physical and mental ravages caused by syphilis and gonorrhea. Condoms were standard Government Issue along with cigarettes. Fear and love of me were enough to make waiting several years possible for Phil.

In 1942-1946, I had fears of the consequences of intercourse. Rumors of a pregnant Smith girl hanging herself and coat hanger abortions were on my mind. I was influenced by the fact that I was Head of the Honor Board and on the Student Council at Smith. Rules were important to me. I was a straight arrow.

The alternative would have been to get married while in college as many classmates did, but we had opted to wait until I graduated. Stopping at heavy petting was possible because we were separated most of the time by Army service and college.

In 1946 we got married. The preferred and popular birth control method given to me by my doctor in a premarital visit was the diaphragm, a soft rubber cap for the cervix fitted by a doctor to be insert for each encounter. Leaving this at home while on a camping trip ended in the joyful pregnancy and the birth of our beloved Martha a year after our marriage. I think now that the urge to reproduce was strong for all WWII couples. Hence the baby boom. She was a wanted baby. We were thrilled.

The diaphragm helped with the spacing of our other wonderful children, sons Art and Ben. Birth control itself was illegal until the Supreme Court Ruling on the case of Griswold v. Connecticut, but a doctor's prescription allowed me, the affluent and educated, to practice. Believing that this was the right of all women, I volunteered at Planned Parenthood after our move to St. Louis. In our late thirties, a strong urge developed to have a fourth child. We had had wonderful experience and fun with our three. We had money saved up for their college educations. We felt young and vigorous. After much debate and professional counseling for me, we decided it was a joyous go. First there was a miscarriage and then our beloved Warren at age forty.

Warren was born in 1966. The pill was now the preferred method of birth control affording new freedom and spontaneity for us, controlling the size of our family until I had a hysterectomy in 1976. Hormone replacement therapy kept my libido in top condition. The pill and the hysterectomy were greatly liberating. Looking back, it is easy for me to see how the pill caused the sexual revolution of the sixties. During this period, we read many books and among the biggest revelation was that the brain is our most important sex organ. This encouraged us to think of sex as a healthy wonderful gift that could be discussed in words. This enabled us to learn that we needed to communicate our own needs and pleasures openly. We were able to see that while we were wonderful partners we were not responsible for each other's fulfillment.

We read and discussed a huge variety of books together from the "The Joy of Sex" to "Lady Chatterley's Lover", "The Marquis de Sade", "Lolita" and many unremembered. We tried things to satisfy our curiosity in the safety of our own bedroom, but in later years or what some people may call old age or the senior years we decided that the old fashioned missionary position was best for us. In senior years, we actually scheduled sex for every Saturday morning with no exceptions or discussion. Actually, these octogenarian experiences were the best - a true physical, spiritual sublime union.

Chapter 6. Princeton

1946 - 1948 Age 21 - 23

At age 89 I mused, have I ever done anything historic, anything that was first? Yes, I have. I was a woman that spent the whole summer session of 1946 sleeping and living in Brown Hall at Princeton University, a bastion of male supremacy. This was years and years before women were admitted to Princeton. How did I do this? I married a recently returned World War II veteran Princeton student Phil Wood, class of '46. Veterans' housing was not yet ready, and so as bride and groom, a week after our wedding in June, 1946 we climbed to the 4th floor of Brown with all of our earthly possessions - mostly impractical expensive wedding presents and books but very light on pots, pans, towels or practical items.

I was a seasoned dorm dweller and dorm lover since I had just graduated from Smith College ten days before. However, I was not a seasoned perfect housewife and that was what I enthusiastically aspired to be. Smith honors studies in political science, student government and heading and founding the Honor Board had NOT prepared me for cooking - especially cooking on a one or two burner hot plate. We acquired a metal box which could be set on the hot plate to make an oven. My future mother-in-law had given me "The Joy of Cooking". I attempted recipes like chicken croquettes with wifely dedication. Once the butcher asked me if we were having company for dinner when I bought three slices of bologna. We had an icebox with a drip pan. The iceman's visits were ritual. Our refrigerator was well stocked with beer to share with friends. I remember Phil bounding up the four flights carrying a case of beer while looking so cool in his white bucks, khakis and white Princeton beer jacket always with a huge smile. I shopped daily on foot because of course there was no freezer or frozen food. I loved walking through the verdant campus past historic Nassau Hall to buy my groceries. We had no car. Dishes were washed in a restroom or janitors closet. Wives and husbands used alternate floors for bathrooms. I can't remember who was lucky enough to have the fourth floor. Our kitchen table was the card table, a wedding present. We used our Tiffany silver rather than spend money for stainless. We even entertained for dinner.

I can still see our living room with a cot and pillows for a sofa with a large tole tray (wedding present) as a coffee

table and planters and vases filled with ivy from the
outdoor walls, wedding pictures from our elegant wedding
and wedding silver - no easy chair but we loved it. My
grandfather gave us money for our first double bed. We
never wanted a bigger bed in all of our almost 68 married
years, although upgrading to a stove and refrigerator was a
happy event.

I was a married woman now. Therefore, I traded my Smith
College blue jeans for a pink wrapper house dress when I
was home in our Brown Hall suite. I also loved to wear my
white satin wedding negligee at home in a quick transition
from a college girl wearing sensible PJs to post war WIFE
awaiting employment at Miss Fine's School in the fall. I
did laundry in the bathroom sinks. Domesticity did
completely capture me that summer which was good
because the Princeton library was not open to wives. Phil
meantime was loving his courses, professors and
academia.

Occasionally, a few undergraduates would bound through
the open windows via fire escapes. We thought these antics
and pranks lots of fun. We laughed a lot. I liked sharing a
floor with other couples and brushing my teeth with other
wives was a friendly dormitory touch. Our Brown Hall
experience was a treasure that could only have happened in
1946 at the end of World War II. We were married - a
dream that had only been the stuff of wartime love letters.

Our only issue and cause for disagreement were the invitations from Phil's unmarried friends for him to go out and have a beer and some male fun. Fortunately, four years of developing verbal communication during our courtship had prepared us for civil and thoughtful discourse. We agreed that I would be included in all social life. We set the pattern then. There were never any evening girls' or boys' nights out (except on the road for business). We were best friends and buddies as well as husband and wife. This was an important agreement for us.

Brown Hall reverted to a regular men's dormitory at the end of the summer term. Veterans' housing was not yet ready. So we rented part of the downstairs of a lovely old house on Dickenson Street near the graduate school. The big difference was there was NO COOKING. We traded the hot plate for bikes which we rode to dinners (yum) at Colonial Club which Phil had joined, the Balt, Lahiere's, and the diner outside of town on the highway. I started teaching middle school social studies at very nearby Miss Fine's School - an idyllic setting where my motivated, interested students reported that a nearby neighbor Albcrt Einstein had helped them with homework. My students' fathers were mostly professors. Phil was excitedly studying under some of them - especially loving the preceptorial system with discussion and small group attention. We qualified as chaperones at Colonial Club on football weekends as 21-year-olds because we were married.

The most exciting event of our tenure on Dickenson Street was the discovery that I was pregnant. Except for a little drowsiness at the beginning, I felt wonderful and we were joyous - enhanced by the natural excitement of creating new life after a war. Red and gold autumn leaves, bike riding, Phil's stimulating Princeton courses with A's as marks, teaching, great meals out, and a baby on board made this an idyllic semester still remembered vividly. As Robert Frost said "the green is gold."

Princeton home number three was the Harrison Street Veterans' project, supposed to be temporary, but still looking good at the 60th reunion. News in 2015 is that it is being torn down. We really nested here - a stove, (cooking again) an icebox, an inherited spinner washing machine and an effective kerosene space heater made our 2 bedroom dwelling worthy of fixing up with comfortable slipcovered pieces from a deceased great uncle and curtains sewn by Phil. A beautiful crib from my parents plus bathinette completed the waiting nursery. Phil planted a display of geraniums and morning glories never to be rivaled again during the gardening history of our marriage. Biking to work at school and university classes kept us fit and happy until in my 8th month, a parent who lived nearby drove me.

Martha, a beautiful blue eyed eight pound girl, was born in the Princeton hospital where there was a waiting line for the delivery room because of the post war baby boom. We were in sync with the popular culture of the time. Our vets' housing project was the perfect first home. An expert baby nurse, Mrs. Lebsa, lived in the neighborhood. She took care of many of the project babies with a bath and advice every day. She dispelled every anxiety. I could enjoy classmates from Smith, now mothers pushing baby carriages around the project twice a day. Phil took to fatherhood with enthusiasm, precision, and skill - fastening diapers so neatly, burping so scientifically, pushing the wheeled bassinet back and forth while he savored history chemistry, art and philosophy making straight A's. We all babysat for each other in the project- an ideal place to have a first child. Dr. Spock was our Bible which we read and discussed together practically daily.

I put teaching on hold for more than twenty years, and Phil supplemented our income by tutoring and working at football games. We bought a car - a tiny Crosley. Two sets of New Jersey grandparents visited often and doted on our little princess.

Originally a chemistry major with a desire to become an M.D., Phil's interests detoured toward history, art history, philosophy and French, making career choices many. He was offered and seriously considered a position teaching history in a nearby prep school where we would have been dorm parents. He contemplated going to grad school to pursue his love of history of art which had been ignited in Florence, Italy after the war. He had successful interviews with and offers from recruiters who flooded the postwar campus from corporations like Minnesota Mining and Merck. We ultimately decided on using his chemistry major at Union Carbide Corp in the plastics division headed by my father's best friend. All of our parents were very happy with this decision. We were too.

Being in Princeton with the G.I. Bill to pay for all college with a generous monthly allowance was a two year paradise ending with Phil's graduation in 1948 at age 23. A world class liberal education with majors in both chemistry and history with significant French and art history prepared Phil well for his role as a member of the Greatest Generation. In later years, he remembered the slogan "Princeton in the Nation's Service" as he became a local elected official.

Princeton became especially important to Phil and me again after our move to Tulsa in 1974. Phil served as president of the Princeton Club twice. We enjoyed entertaining the club in our home and attending reunions. Best and most fun of all was organizing a Princeton-Smith Class of 1946 mini reunion in Tulsa in 1999 to showcase

Gilcrease and Philbrook Museums, Art Deco, symphony, Pawhuska with stained glass windows and Osage culture, lecture by a Cherokee, the symphony and more. We had a wonderful time at the 50th and 60th reunions as Phil served as a regional class VP. We liked the new Princeton with women and racial diversity better.

Our friends from the Tulsa Princeton Club have been stalwarts of support for me after Phil's death. I feel warmth and acceptance to ease my nostalgia as I attend parties and meetings alone. Princeton friends were among the first to visit me with cookies after Phil's death. Princeton people care.

Princeton is large in my life as I continue to receive checks from "The Philip and Emily Wood Charitable Remainder Annuity Trust," which we established in 2003 with a relatively small amount. The excellent, unsurpassed Princeton management of the fund has resulted in great growth making it our best investment ever. It will be the completion of a circle started when a seventeen year old boy arrived awaiting the World War II draft and will end with the death of his aged wife.

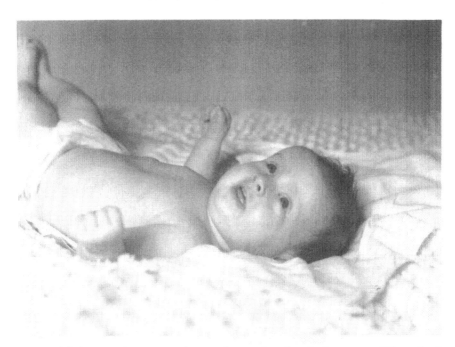

Beautiful Martha Wood was born in the Princeton Hospital in true baby boom style. There was a line-up for the delivery room and an upbeat collegial excitement at the hospital. The happy veterans were back and babies abounded. We were thrilled. The delivery was easy. I was in great shape from all my bike riding. Phil was an enthusiastic cloth diaper changer, burper, bather and loving Daddy.

We took Martha home to the newly completed Harrison Street Veterans' project. We were elated to nest. In this picture, Phil is shown polishing our newly purchased Crosley, a mini-car, our first motorized vehicle. I shudder now when I think of transporting Martha in it in 1940s car seats.

Martha was pushed daily in a fine carriage around the "Project" as Emily socialized with other perambulating mothers. This was a wonderful time in our lives.

Chapter 7. Corporate Training
1948 - 1949 Age 23 - 24

In 1948, at age twenty-three, we left our cozy love nest In
Princeton to begin Phil's one-and-a-half year training for
technical representative at Union Carbide Corporation. Our
elders urged housing in two very large underused
dwellings in our home town of Chatham, New Jersey. This
was a period of great joy and growth, but also a time where
we saw the dark and fearful side of life. It was a time of
firsts - first job and first vote.

Phil was very happy as corporate trainee. He bonded with
his fellow trainees, enjoyed the work, his bosses and a
paycheck with great benefits. We had immediate
insurance, savings plans and retirement plans from day
one. As twenty-three year olds, we had incredible financial
security practically guaranteed until corporate retirement.
The financial stars were well-aligned for the veterans and

their young families when they graduated debt free from first rate universities. At twenty-three, we had a head start predicting my excellent financial situation today because of the G.I. bill and the post war corporate paternalism.

Happy memories of cute toddler Martha thriving with the love of adoring grandparents and aunts, playing with her cousins and riding her Kiddie Car are with me today. We spent the summer in the large home of best friend Chuck Drake's traveling mother. We were attended by Frank, family retainer of years, gardener, and houseman and watchdog extraordinaire. The house was directly across the street from Phil's boyhood home and the then home of Phil's sister and family. My sister, a college student home for the summer, often came bearing vegetables from my father's garden and to eat dinner with us and Chuck, a graduate student at Columbia. Each evening, Chuck and Phil enjoyed playing croquet on the beautifully manicured lawn while little Martha watched. We would then have a garden fresh vegetable dinner on a beautiful porch after a gin and tonic. I took Martha with me to my parents' country club to the pool. It was a beautiful summer.

Mrs. Drake came back and we moved to my grandfather's house, a very large home surrounded by four enormous glass porches reflecting his greenhouse building career. I had lived in this house until I was five when my parents built their own residence across a large green space which was originally part of great-grandfather's farm on family land going back to the Revolutionary War. I spent many childhood hours each week in this house making scrapbooks of newspaper brides, helping my grandmother wash her vast collection of amber glass (some of which I still enjoy today), and pumping the player piano. I also loved her depression 1930s food of rice pancakes and chicken fricassee. I joined both grandparents in their nightly ritual of radio listening to Amos and Andy, popular in the 30s and now known to be racially stereotypical in the worst sense.

We went to live with my widower grandfather, with no apprehension or premonitions of the darkness to follow. Phil, Martha and I settled into two bedrooms, sitting room and bath up the front staircase in the very long spacious house. Pop Pop (Lincoln Pierson) was ensconced, as he had been for sixty years in his master bedroom up the back stairs. It was separate and private. Martha could ride her trike through the endless porches and downstairs rooms. We could wander through the vast treed acreage with houses owned by many kin. Phil went to Union Carbide each day.

For the first few months, Pop Pop slept in his chair downstairs most of the time, seemingly appropriate behavior for an octogenarian. Then he woke with a huge explosive force with almost twenty-four hour energy devoted to having dozens of pictures framed, developing plans for selling land and visiting blueprint makers, cleaning out kitchen cabinets, pruning bushes, wanting to purchase the most exotic foods, ordering fresh flowers, foraging for wild mushrooms, crying over his baby son who died eighty years before, contracting for maintenance chores around the house, demanding that Phil hang pictures and do a myriad of things after work etc. He often threatened to kill his former partner in the rose business who had foreclosed on him, leaving him without income and only his house and land as assets. I was very upset by these outbursts, which usually occurred when Phil was at work.

Grandfather Lincoln's urgent demands for me to borrow my mother's car to take him on errands left me anxious and angry but unable to express it to him. He also demanded perfect exotic melons and gourmet dinners. After work, Phil was good at listening to my complaints and being a reassuring presence. My twenty-three year old working husband Phil became a master of calm communication with my eighty year old manic grandfather. Phil set up a regular meeting time twice a week. By the time of the meeting, all the demands were forgotten. Phil also could say NO to him in a very pleasant voice.

Phil's most important and calmest NO came when Pop Pop picked a large number of wild mushrooms and ordered emphatically that the three of us eat them, stating with certainty that the toadstools were not poisonous. Phil and I did not join him in eating the fungi.

During the night, grandfather became violently ill with his loud moans and cries audible from his distant quarters. We called his doctor and his daughters, one of whom was my mother. The doctor arrived quickly and predicted probable death stating there was no remedy. Phil and I retired leaving him in the care of his daughters. When Phil left for work, Pop Pop had cooked himself a large egg breakfast and was out cutting brush.

Now it is clear that my grandfather was exhibiting the symptoms of manic depression or bipolar disease and was mentally ill. His daughters, my aunts and my mother, said he always exhibited pronounced highs and lows during his very creative life of greenhouse designer and builder for the robber barons of a bygone era. These symptoms had been exacerbated by old age. His daughters were sorry that they suggested we live with him. The experience made me realize the horrors of untreated mental illness. In this day and age, medication can alleviate bipolar symptoms. The present day tragedy is that diagnosis and treatment are financially unavailable to so many. The stress on families often causes homelessness. If we hadn't lived with Pop

Pop, I might not understand that today. I know I was very happy to be able to leave. Phil was a bridge across troubled waters. He communicated effectively with Pop Pop. He communicated calm and reason to me. He took care of himself and his own. He was my rock. Phil taught me that taking care of myself and Martha was of prime importance. Above all, he listened to my complaints, and listening is the highest form of communication.

We had passed the twenty-one year old voting age mark and could vote in our first presidential election. We voted for Republican Thomas Dewey, the New York prosecutor who cleaned up corruption. If I could vote in this election again today, I would definitely vote for Harry Truman who desegregated the armed forces and started the Marshall Plan to rebuild postwar Europe.

While living at Pop Pop's, we decided that we wanted a second child because we enjoyed parenthood so much. I was happily pregnant when we left for St. Louis, Phil's first field assignment. We were optimistic and excited about the future.

Martha and I enjoyed much outdoor time on the beautiful lawns at Pop Pop's. Dog, Strudel, belonged to my sister after whom Martha is named.

Martha at Pop Pop's in a 1949 snowstorm. Fresh air, fresh cooked hot meals with lamb chops and veggies, naps and very early bedtime were child raising rules then.

While living at Pop Pop's, Martha visited Nanny Ruth and Grampy Art constantly. They adored her, their first grandchild.

Chapter 8. St. Louis Route 66

1950 - 1953 Ages 25 - 28

When Phil and I celebrated our sixty-sixth wedding
anniversary in 2012, we ate at Tally's Route 66 Diner in
Tulsa. The previous year we had taken our grandsons,
Sami and Zane, on a Route 66 historic tour to Oklahoma
City, stopping at sites like Pops, the Round Barn and
various museums where we sampled replicas of old motel
rooms and other venues. In previous years, we had often
taken Route 66 past the Blue Whale in Catoosa, the totem
poles in Chelsea and on to Afton en route to Grand Lake.
Thinking about the Mother Road reminded me of our three
years in St. Louis, 1950-1953.

Union Carbide Corporation assigned Phil to St. Louis. We
arrived with our beautiful two-and-a-half-year-old Martha
with unbounded post-war optimism about our role in
corporate America. I was joyously pregnant. World War
Two left Phil with the feeling that all of the United States

was our hometown. I was the first to leave my family's seven generation pre-Revolutionary War acreage in New Jersey to embrace the idea of being a latter-day Western pioneer. We were embarking on a new adventure together, eager to increase our family and take the first step up the corporate ladder and live the American dream.

We used the G.I. Bill to easily buy a two bedroom, one bath home in Glendale, Missouri (St. Louis suburb) just about a mile south of Manchester Road, Route 66. Little did we know that we were living close to the main street of America. We were living in the midst of Phil's huge sales territory including Missouri, Indiana, Texas, Oklahoma, Louisiana and more. Route 66 was to be traversed many times in his shiny Chevrolet company car. Being "on the road" was a foreign concept to a girl whose father and father-in-law commuted to New York City daily by train and tube or ferry to return every night.

Reality struck when Phil left for a ten day trip to Texas. I had not had time to get to know the neighbors. I had never slept in a house without another adult. I heard ominous news about a gang in Missouri. I was afraid and lonely. I telephoned my father recounting my complaints. His reply was, "You are married to a wonderful man. You have a gorgeous daughter. Your husband has a first class job. You have a wonderful education. You are very lucky and a married woman." I got the strong message that I was the only one who could solve my own problems. It was excellent advice from a very wise father. The next day I called Smith College connections. I invited two of them to my house for lunch and bought a Scottie puppy from the third. I soon was on the board of the St. Louis Smith Club as the secretary. I went out and talked to my neighbors, all young mothers like myself. We became fast friends with our children's welfare in common. I called recommended doctors. I called the uncle and aunt of one of my New Jersey friends who were delighted to become surrogate parents and grandparents to us because their children were away. When Phil came back, Martha, Polly (the puppy) and I were happy St. Louis residents.

Phil drove Route 66 as a Technical Representative for Union Carbide Corporation to supply railroad car after car of raw plastic pellets to RCA, Decca Records in Indiana, and numerous other customers. The miraculous plastics business was brand new with slogans like, "Better living through chemistry." Environmental issues had not yet confronted the world. Excitement abounded as the plastic pellets were turned into records with such recording artists as the new and young Elvis Presley.

Phil's most exciting journey along Route 66 from Indianapolis was for the birth of our second child, Arthur. Art was supposed to be born early in May. My self-assured mother, Ruth, had driven her dear Odessa, household helper, from New Jersey to help us with the birth and stay with Martha. They had avoided the pitfalls of segregation still prevalent in the 1950s. Art was very, very late and inducement was not an option then. Phil stayed off the road. We waited and waited.

Mother and Odessa finally had to leave to prepare for my sister's soon scheduled wedding. Phil went back on the road. Since I had no car, I was driven to a Smith College Club meeting by a fellow alum. I called Phil from the meeting saying I thought the baby was coming. When I got home from the meeting, contractions started. I got the babysitter, who arranged for and called a cab. As I left in the taxi, Martha cried and tried to follow, a heart wrenching moment. The cab headed down Route 66 toward St. Luke's Hospital and my next memory is of waking up and seeing Phil with a tomato colored tie and tan summer suit smiling down at me. He had sped across 66 from Indianapolis to St. Louis and made it for Art's birth to see that we had a very healthy son. We had not known we would have a boy. We were overjoyed to have a son. Once again the Mother Road brought Phil home. Art was a very peaceful, happy baby who was content to sleep and eat with no colicky moments. He was named after a maternal grandfather, a paternal great grandfather and best friend, soon to be brother-in-law Charles Drake.

Four weeks after Art's birth, the four of us were on our way to New Jersey to the wedding of my sister, Martha, and Chuck Drake, Phil's best high school and Princeton friend and now to be brother-in-law. We were traveling in luxury on the Pullman of the Pennsylvania's crack train, Spirit of St. Louis, thanks to the generosity of my parents. Phil carried Art proudly in a beautiful bassinet which we had in our compartment - a perfect setup for travel with baby. Our porter, Jerome, had become a friend to Martha and me when Union Carbide sent us to St. Louis six months before. Riding Pullman was pure pampered comfort. Now that there were four of us it was pure joy. This was a perk of corporate life and corporate moves that I enjoyed several times. We got to New Jersey, Martha's old baby nurse from Princeton was there to help during the wedding, a duplicate of our wedding four years before produced by my parents, who loved Chuck as much as they loved Phil. Chuck became a world renowned geophysicist.

Back in St. Louis after our trip, Phil often headed west on Route 66 to Tulsa to market his plastics. He remembered a hot ride in the summer before air conditioning and staying in a motel, which was decrepit by 1974 when we moved to Tulsa, and torn down sometime in the 80s. As an alternate, he sometimes took the train to Tulsa to the beautiful station that is now the Oklahoma Jazz Hall of Fame.

On weekends in St. Louis on Route 66, we experienced a new, unknown and wondrous family treat, the Steak and Shake Drive-In. Sunday afternoons saw the four of us in the company car on the Mother Road heading for the monkey show at the zoo, the beautiful Jewel Box in Forest Park or the Botanical Gardens, which were special because my grandfather Lincoln Pierson had designed and sold the UBar Green House on a trip from the East. Art loved the statues in the art museum and was fascinated by toes, which he called piggies.

Phil had a small office in nearby Kirkwood where he had a secretary to do paper work in pre-computer times. He also had some customers in St. Louis, but most weeks he was on the road Tuesday, Wednesday and Thursday nights. We missed him, but had wonderful neighbors during that era. All of us were stay-at-home moms who visited constantly with coffees and yard visits. All the children played on our dead end street. Martha watched Howdy Doody, something completely new to me, on our dear neighbor's screen. Phil's homecomings each week were a joyous occasion with all housework done and a gleaming house to welcome him. His homecoming combined honeymoon and family feelings of love. It was the 1950s.

The lure of a vice presidency at age twenty-five in a Princeton family plastics business provided a luxurious company car and many beautiful experiences with the elite of St. Louis for an interlude of about a year and a half. When Phil realized that even though he was treated very well, he was not family, he decided to try to go back to Union Carbide. I cried tears of fear and was scared initially. His employers valued him and gave us the company car and vacation time to go to Florida to think it over. Martha and Arthur loved the Florida beach and I dried my tears. He went back to Union Carbide Corporation in NY for more training before reassignment. Never again would we live so close to Route 66 until we moved to Tulsa eighteen years later.

Visiting from St. Louis. Emily, Baby Art, Martha, with Grampy Art. We came to New Jersey for the wedding of sister Martha Churchill and Chuck Drake. We travelled by Pullman on the Spirit of St. Louis with Daddy Phil. Art was also named for Great Grandfather Arthur Wood.

Emily holds Arthur, a handsome boy, when he was about a year old on a visit to Granddaddy Ernest and Grandma Dee Dee in Brookside, New Jersey. Phil drove us from St. Louis. President Eisenhower's Interstate initiative had not been implemented.

Season's Greetings

from our house to your house

St. Louis Christmas, 1951. Dog Polly, Martha and Art.
Dog Polly was purchased from a Smith College friend
immediately after we arrived in St. Louis. No fireplace but
lots of love! Art was a big, happy, smiling boy.

Chapter 9. Back to Union Carbide and Michigan
1953-1956 Ages 28-31

In 1953, Phil returned to the giant Union Carbide via a New York retraining period with amazing alacrity and energy. I took over all moving details with the efficiency, confidence and enthusiasm of a dedicated company wife, a role which I embraced with ardor. Communication between us was concise and clear and directed to the return to corporate trajectory, but also laced with love of our growing family and our marital partnership. It was the 1950s.

We were planning a third child. We loved being parents. Martha finished a very successful kindergarten year at the nearby public school in St. Louis. She and her teacher, Miss Goosetree, had a mutual admiration relationship which was celebrated when Miss G. came to dinner at our house with Martha as hostess in her best velvet dress. I engineered a sixth birthday party which was also sayonara to the many neighborhood play pals and their parents.

In the midst of readying the house for sale, some turpentine was left on the porch. Three year old Art spilled it, but I took him to Barnes Hospital to make sure that he had not swallowed any. A stomach pump confirmed he had not. I stayed calm and in control. I stored the furniture and sold the house, freeing Phil to work back East. I relished my key role in our partnership. My eye was still on the corporate ladder. It was the 1950s.

Martha, Art, Polly and I headed back to Chatham, New Jersey to large Victorian home belonging to Mrs. Drake where we had once lived and were so ably attended by retainer Frank. We joyously joined Phil who was an eager Union Carbide employee again. It was a summer of swimming, visiting grandparents at a rented Cape Cod cottage and playing with cousins across the street while Phil worked. In the fall, Martha walked down the street to Phil's old school for first grade and easily mastered the reader of the 1950s, Dick and Jane. Her printing was beautiful. Her first grade teacher walked home with her for lunch on the beautiful Victorian porch. Art attended a very familiar nursery school a few blocks up the street established when Phil was young. The director reported that Art was amazingly well-adjusted and happy for a three year old who had just been moved. All four NJ grandparents doted on the children. It was a peaceful time marred only by Polly's defecation on a priceless oriental rug in the Drake dining room. Subsequent conversation with Frank left me apologetic, anxious and watchful. Pop Pop was now in a nursing home with his big home sold.

In November, Phil was assigned to a large territory centered in Michigan. He set off by car right after Thanksgiving to meet our furniture coming from storage in St. Louis at a rental house just abandoned by his work predecessor. Martha, Art, Puppy Polly, and new kitten, Butterball and I were sent by Pullman compartment, courtesy of the company, to meet Phil in South Bend, Indiana. My dear, efficient mother drove us to NYC Grand Central station, parked and helped us board. All was smooth except Butterball's anxious scratches delivered to all humans. After a dining car dinner, the children donned their feet pajamas and we went to the club car, leaving the animals in our bed chamber. The adorable youngsters were the darlings of all the businessmen traveling. I had a good time.

Traveling on a crack train between New York and Chicago was luxurious fun for me. The next morning when we got off the train in South Bend, there was our always smiling Phil standing in the falling snow. After hugs and kisses, we were off to the Benton Harbor/St. Joseph, Michigan area. We spent the night in the most luxurious hotel that the community offered, a company perk which I loved.

The three bedroom, one and a half bath, two story house fronted on a triangular park which was replete with state of the art playground equipment. The high ceilings accommodated the very large fresh Christmas tree with a circle of electric trains. We were excited by the fireplace. We bought our first TV, which was basically a tin box. Phil converted a moving carton into a playhouse painted like a Swiss chalet. He acquired many children's records from RCA and Decca where he was back selling carloads of plastic. Art's favorite was Old Witch Who Lived in a Ditch. Three year old Art played it over and over as he danced joyously in his feet pajamas.

Three weeks after moving to Michigan we celebrated a wonderful Christmas. Immediately upon our arrival, the minister, and his wife, of a large Congregational church called on us. Through them, I had an instant and large support system and friends. I immediately had lists of doctors, babysitters, nursery schools, play groups, bridge groups etc. and support for the upcoming birth of Ben. The minister and his wife were attentive hospital visitors when Ben, a sparkling, energetic, adorable boy was born in May. He was a smiling, curious dynamo who walked at nine months, started talking soon after and at an early age developed a penchant for climbing and tools. By the time he was one, he had a fast friend who lived behind us. They were two toddler fixtures in the park with mothers (I, of course, was one) who became fast friends. Martha and Art found wonderful playmates and life was happy around Napier Park.

Phil was on the road three nights a week, but he had plenty of time to skate, sled, and swim with Martha and Arthur. Our church friends invited us to join the St. Joseph yacht Club with dues of $25 dollars (it had been the home of the Uptons, founders of Whirlpool, who continued to subsidize it). We had many wonderful family pancake breakfasts there with Ben in his carriage on the broad fine sand beach and many large family hamburger parties on the beach as the sun set over Lake Michigan as well as wonderful swims. The Whirlpool Corporation was Phil's best customer buying all the raw plastics for the many, many washing machine agitators that were flooding post war America. Swimming lessons at the club and in the winter at the nearby Y turned our children into great swimmers. I was Martha's Brownie leader, a Sunday school teacher and a hospital play lady through the church. I was very happy. I still have friends there.

We also saw a lot of our family from the East. One summer we drove with the rickety car seats of the day to Cape Cod for a beach vacation with my parents and sister's family. We stopped at Niagara Falls where holding on to active toddler Ben was a challenge. My brother was a jet pilot stationed in nearby Wisconsin. We visited with Phil's brother, then on the faculty of the University of Michigan, and Phil's parents spent several weeks with us. We were not lonely. We also were quite insular in the 1950s. I remember the McCarthy hearings and not being enraged as I was later when I taught American History. I remember picking up an African American house worker in a ghetto section of town and accepting it unemotionally. I am not proud of my go along 1950s ways.

Phil had done a wonderful job with large customers like RCA and Whirlpool and was tapped to become a Zone Sales Manager with a sales force of six men, and then shortly after that he was made Regional Manager for the Bakelite Division of Union Carbide in Chicago involving a family move. He went ahead to the luxurious offices at 230 Michigan Avenue where the sixty year old longtime office manager was called Mae whereas the thirty-two year old Phil was called Mr. Wood as he settled into his very large office with the requisite mahogany desk. The children and I loved train rides so we took the ninety mile train ride down the shores of Lake Michigan to meet daddy to look for a house. Again hugs and excitement and a weekend, thanks to the company, at the fancy Edgewater Beach Hotel with a swaying bridge to delight the young.

We wanted a house in the legendary New Trier School District. We lived in a modest house, but with the highest taxes we have ever paid to this day. Quality education is not cheap. Union Carbide arranged all the details of this move. I had what I had been wishing for - a big step up the corporate ladder. I was the boss's wife and the boss was very preoccupied with being the boss. Our communication was beginning to falter. It was the 1950s - and we were in Chicago.

Phil with Union Carbide railroad car of plastic pellets. Phil, as a technical representative, sold thousands of railroad cars of plastic pellets to RCA and Decca Records to record such artists as the emerging Elvis Presley. I urged him on as he became a zone and regional manager.

Emily and Ben in Benton Harbor in 1954. Ben did not sit long. He walked and climbed ladders at 9 months! He also talked very early!

Ben, born in May, joined Martha and Arthur for a 1954
Christmas in Michigan. Ben sparkled as a baby.

On vacation, Cape Cod, 1955. We drove from Michigan before the Interstates. Memorable was stopping at Niagara Falls and holding on to active one year old Ben. We visited my parents at a rented cottage to be with cousins, uncles and aunts.

Chapter 10. Chicago
1956 - 1960 Ages 31-35

Now I will flash forward 59 years. On August 1, 2015,
Swiss Independence Day, I arrived at the Swissotel in
Chicago with my beloved Tulsa family (son Warren, wife
Abir, grandsons Sami and Zane) for a weekend filled with
memories. Warren and I remembered sitting on the shores
of Lake Geneva in Switzerland during a backpacking
Alpine adventure with Phil as the Flugelhorns celebrated
the national holiday. The five of us immediately went for
lunch and sat at a six seat, white-clothed round table. There
was a sixth chair, empty. It was a metaphor for Phil's
legacy of fun, gracious hosting and perpetual check
paying. We missed our dear Phil, Dad and Papa.

A post lunch perambulation took us past the impressive
Carbide and Carbon building on Michigan Avenue where
Phil first became a "boss" of an office which had not yet
been transformed by the feminist movement of the 1960s.

All the men were called Mister even if they were twenty-two years old. All of the women (girls) were called by their first names and were secretaries. Wives were all stay-at-home mothers. I was titled the boss's wife. Male camaraderie and morale were very high. Expense accounts were generous. Mayor Daley and Hugh Hefner of Playboy fame were the political and cultural icons. It was the 1950s.

Our suburban home was very close to the train that Phil took downtown, although he still retained his company car. Our neighborhood was safe with children and pets roaming and playing out of doors freely. The public schools were excellent. The park district included summer swimming in Lake Michigan and winter rink ice-skating which we loved. Extremely high real estate taxes supported this life style. We were thirty-two years old. It was the 1950s.

On Sunday nights, our family of five ritual was to gather in the basement rec room to watch Jack Benny, Leave it to Beaver, and Father Knows best. Earlier in the day, we had attended the local Community Christian Church and often played board games like Candyland in front of the fire. We also regularly went to the Chicago museums with the Museum of Science and Industry being a favorite. We had a Scotty dog pet and Art had a rabbit, Elvis. It was the 1950s.

I aspired to be like June Cleaver, the mother in "Leave it to Beaver." Washing, shopping and cake baking were done when Phil was at work, leaving at home hours for family meals and fun. The only trouble was that I wasn't June Cleaver. I occasionally got angry when Phil was late for dinner because of customers and dinners with his team. I was ashamed of my anger because we had it all. It was the 1950s.

I got very tired for the first time in my life. My boundless energy was gone. I went to the doctor who found nothing physically wrong but said he was seeing this syndrome of tired thirty year old mothers/wives repeatedly. He sent me to a psychiatrist who jokingly said, "You getting bedsores from resting?" He reminded me that I had stopped expressing my wants and needs in words. Anger unexpressed turned to fatigue. The mind body connection became obvious. He prescribed dancing lessons and dates for the two of us. One month later, I was a new person. I was communicating my needs again without the company wife guilt. We started dancing together and continued for fifty-five years. The waltz was our favorite. Phil was very good at counting 1, 2, 3. I was happy and energized again. It was the 1950s.

I do not remember the names of either the doctor or the psychiatrist, but I thank them with all my heart for a diagnosis and life lesson which has served me so well for fifty-eight years. Business flourished. Wives were included in more activities. As a family, we celebrated holidays with our neighbors and camped with them with probably too much alcohol. Phil was the troop chair for Arthur's Cub Scout Troop. I went on Girl Scout campouts with Martha. Ben had great neighborhood pals. Art dug large holes with neighborhood friends in the nearby forest preserve. Phil bought a nine foot sailboat to sail in the nearby lagoons. We were Republicans and I volunteered at the polls. It was the 1950s.

However, I was happy and energized because I did not think that I had to be June Cleaver and that Father Did Not always Know Best. The 1950s were giving way to the 60s. Martha, who was in seventh grade had a Beatnik party at our house predicting what was to come. The 1950s were ending.

Phil and I were talking, loving and dancing. We had learned that culture and times change, but communication is the key in any decade.

1960s, Union Carbide Manager in Plastics Division.

Ben, Martha and Art were dressed up for Sunday School on Easter after the egg hunt in Chicago suburb. Phil treated us to a fancy Easter Brunch. We also went to museums, zoos and parks in Chicago constantly.

Ben got both a doctor kit and a giant Teddy Bear for Christmas. We had legendary Christmas celebrations.

Art and Ben played together with many neighborhood friends in Chicago. Mart was an active Scout.

Phil carving the Thanksgiving turkey. Traditional holidays
were important to our little family. It was the 1950s.

Chapter 11. Larchmont

1960 - 1974 Ages 35-49

In 1960, Phil was transferred to Union Carbide Headquarters in New York City. In the middle of the year, we removed our children from their happy place at the excellent Avoca Elementary School. Looking back now as a forty-five year veteran teacher, I realize this was a significant childhood event. Perhaps, since Phil and I never moved as children, we did not comprehend what a difficult change this could be. I apologize to them now, but also applaud them for making friends quickly and working hard for academic success.

The corporation made the physical act of moving easy. We reveled in train travel with luxurious family sleeping arrangements. We arrived at Grand Central Station, a place of happy memories, and went to a first class hotel to await the moving van. This was a fun family time. Union Carbide bought our Illinois house and moved/packed everything from a toothbrush to our sailboat and old black Chevrolet car. Amid high snow drifts, the movers trudged through our narrow four story house on a fifty foot lot leaving all in its proper place with all packing material removed. All was planned, paid for and professionally executed by the corporation as was the custom of 1960. For me, it was an adventure to ride the rails and stay in hotels.

The affordable house Phil and I picked out was on a dead end street around the corner from an excellent elementary school and within easy walking distance of stores (grocery, drug, book, clothing, gift, toy, shoe, bakery), tantalizing restaurants, a magnificent beach and rocky waterfront park and the railroad station. We loved to walk!

We were instantly embraced by our friendly neighbors who invited us for a welcoming dinner even before the moving van pulled away. The large population of boys on the block became instant friends for our Art and Ben, but the street was devoid of girls near Martha's age. An eighth grader, she also entered a large junior high with many factions (a real change from her small K-8 school). She handled this daunting situation amazingly well with the help of Girl Scouts and a much loved summer camp.

I immediately became active and soon was a board member of the Newcomers Club, the Junior League and the League of Women voters where I concentrated on publicity and editing. Phil commuted daily (35 minutes to Grand Central, spent reading the New York Times with a five minute covered walk to 270 Park Avenue), but in the evenings and on weekends found time for the Larchmont Nature Council, eventually becoming its president with clean water advocacy for Long Island Sound. As a family, we attended the Unitarian Church in White Plains. We played in a duplicate bridge group, were co-leaders of Martha's Mariner Scout troop and Phil was the Pack Master of Ben's Cub Scouts. We had many friends and were fully engaged in the community.

Art and Ben waited on the sidewalk curb to welcome their beloved commuter Dad after his five minute walk from the station. Following an adult cocktail, on week nights we enjoyed a candle light all family dinner in the dining room around the table, even if the entrée was macaroni/tuna casserole. Our discussions were lively with frequent reinforcement from the encyclopedia. It was the 1960's and the family dinner was a treasured time when father returned from work prepared by stay-at-home mom. In the heavenly Larchmont summers, a picnic following a swim at the beach often replaced the dining room in the evening.

All three children took sailing lessons at the beautiful Horseshoe Harbor Yacht Club bringing home lots of silver. These special times in this beautiful rocky cove were remembered on July 7, 2013, when grandson Jason and

girlfriend Amy brought a portion of Phil's ashes from Tulsa
to be released into Phil's much loved waters by
Martha, Ben, and Warren as I watched with grandsons
Sami and Zane. We remembered how Phil relished
launching the South Sea Proa from the harbor with Art and
Ben. Art worked tirelessly with his Dad to produce this
amazing craft.

Phil's ashes started their journey in the currents that might
lead them to a distant shore while I remembered Saturday
dates when the two of us took a long sail to City Island for
lunch in our nine foot craft. I could hear him commanding,
"Ready About" and me squealing, "Oh, Phil" as a large
barge approached. The sail was an adventure where we
worked as one to avoid capsizing. These sails were a
beautiful metaphor for our life - working in harmony to
solve problems.

Vacations brought pure family adventure time on camping
trips in New Jersey, Pennsylvania, New York, and Florida
state parks as we survived tropical storms sleeping on
bumpy coral in a tent and frigid temperatures in lean-tos.
These camping trips were often combined with visits to
Civil War battlefields, plantations and other historic sights.
Holidays such as Easter and Thanksgiving were often spent
at large, fun, bounteous celebrations with extended family
in nearby New Jersey. Cold weather often found us on a
family trip to a NYC museum, gallery, or ethnic restaurant

or ice skating on a frozen local pond. Phil and I loved these
family times. We felt it was a good life.

Our three children did well in school progressing to and
through Mamaroneck High School with many activities.
Martha graduated in 1965 with a strong academic
background and many experiences ranging from Concert
Choir to class officer. She matriculated as a third generation
student at Smith College with an art major and worked as
an excellent waitress at several restaurants. Low point was
when a fellow employee drilled a hole for spying on her in
the ladies room. Art played the tuba and sang in choirs.
Unfortunately, his football career was ended by a very
persistent staph infection. His present disability may be
attributed to the hard bodily contact and inadequate
equipment of that era. His paid jobs included clearing
nature trails, pumping gas at the nearby Mamaroneck
Harbor and working for the U.S. Park Service at Crater
Lake, Oregon. He went on to study forestry at Paul Smith's
College in the Adirondacks and The University of
Massachusetts at Amherst, Mass. Ben excelled in acting in
junior high and was a high school basketball star going on
to Lafayette College (following many great uncles) and the
State University of New York (Phi Beta Kappa) as an
English major who was published in poetry journals and
winning a graduate fellowship at the University of
Minnesota. Summer job for Ben was taxi driving. We
enjoyed visiting all of these colleges.

Phil's career In New York encompassed a variety of tasks.
He headed a plastic bag group in cooperation with the
Cranberry New Jersey Research Center and held a U.S.
Patent on a bag folding process. He traveled to Germany to
buy equipment for the bag making plant, also located in
New Jersey. Phil was elected a director of a milk bag
company in the Netherlands. I accompanied him on a
business trip to Belgium, Holland and England. My first
trip to Europe revealed a magic world of canals, windmills,
crown jewels and so much more. I was thrilled. We were
enjoying our teenage family and a career with financial
security. We were in excellent health and growing more
and more in love wanting to prolong this happiness, so we
talked about having another baby. People were appalled but
we kept talking - even consulting a psychiatrist and made a
very conscious decision that it was a go. One miscarriage
confirmed our desire.

We joyfully welcomed the adorable Warren Thomas Wood
at New Rochelle Hospital on April 3, 1966. Times had
changed since our earlier deliveries and Phil was allowed to
be present for the miracle of the natural birth. I can still
envision his radiant smile. We were 41, the prime of life.
Martha, a freshman at Smith came home at Easter to join
Art, 16, and Ben, 12, in welcoming their new precious
brother. Phil cooked a ham for the joyous family
celebration of our four wonderful children. The older

children turned into loving babysitters. My cup was running over.

We were euphoric. Just before Warren's birth, Cities Service Corporation hired Phil to start a Plastics Division as all the other major oil companies had done. This was a huge professional step forward from manager to executive creating a whole new entity. Phil embraced this opportunity with unbounded enthusiasm and appreciation and was completely ready for this challenge. He continued his commute to New York for the next eight years to work he adored, but also with greatly enhanced financial rewards. A new baby and a new job made for lots of happiness.

Serious communication followed our large financial leap. Guided by our long-established financial policy, we opted for no new elegant house and no new fancy car. Between accrued Union Carbide savings plan and a higher new salary we were able to pay off our entire mortgage, send all three children to college, pay for my Master's degree and afford yard and household help. We never had to worry about finances again until death did us part.

However, the sirens of the rising feminism of the 1960s reached my psyche as I read, "The Feminine Mystique" by fellow Smith Alumna, Betty Friedan. It was the1960s and I was inching away from my June Cleaver image as I substituted research on Taoism in a study group for my reading diet of the Ladies Home Journal. I was conflicted between being the perfect corporate wife and seeking a career identity of my own. I even sought psychiatric help in making the decision. With full support and encouragement from Phil, I enrolled in a Master of Arts in Teaching program at nearby Manhattanville College. The courses were stimulating and interesting, especially the African American History-Literature class. Spreading the study and student teaching over three years allowed me to mother, learn and continue the corporate wife role. It was the best of three worlds and the beginning of an unbelievably rewarding 45 year teaching career. On the weekends, Phil and I often took Warren to roam the beautiful campus. It was a win-win situation.

The years in Larchmont were the best of times, but they were also the worst of times. A terrible tragedy struck for Arthur, newly graduated from the University of Massachusetts. His beloved girlfriend, brutally murdered in Boston, was left by the highway by a killer who was later indicted for several murders. The scars of this horror remain today. Phil and I tried to be supportive, but only now am I beginning to understand grief. We wished we could have helped him more.

The assassinations of John F. Kennedy, Dr. Martin Luther

King, Jr. and Bobby Kennedy as well as the ill-advised Vietnam War were events that rocked the nation and especially its young people. TV brought the grim reality into homes of innocents dying in Selma and being hosed in Birmingham. Our self-absorption of the1950s gave way to a realization of cruel injustices. Phil and I did go on a bus of protesters to Washington. I am ashamed that we did not do more.

Martha won a full scholarship to Harvard Graduate School of Architecture. She left after one year. It was a very troubled time for universities and students who were appalled by inequalities, lack of civil rights for many and conscription to fight in an unjustifiable war.

Warren thrived on the Larchmont home front. His first school was a Montessori school, where he fell in love with math at three years old as he sat on his rug with his hands-on materials. Our dead end street was an ideal place to learn to ride a tricycle and play endlessly with friends. He was watched over by brothers, wonderful au pairs from Australia and Jamaica as well as his parents. Public School brought his introduction to chess.

In 1974, when Warren was eight and Ben a twenty year old college senior, Cities Service moved its headquarters to Tulsa. Phil was completely in accord with this as a sound business decision. Personally, he did not want to leave his beloved Larchmont. I was ready to continue the corporate journey with Cities Service. Much communication between us and a financial incentive to move helped us decide to relocate. The house was sold. The moving van came.

At the time of our move, Martha was married and leading a 1970s, back to the land life. She and her husband pumped water from a well in New Jersey, raising their food with a pig, chickens and gardens. Art married after entering the millwork business in New Jersey and acquired a beautiful, intelligent five-year-old daughter, Cynde making us happy grandparents. Ben was a senior at the State University of New York, Stony Brook.

We arrived in Tulsa in the summer heat of August 1974. The house which we bought had been renovated and redecorated and was on a large lot. Neighbors greeted us with lemonade. Phil was a seven minute drive from work. I had a job in an excellent learning disabilities school. Warren's nearby Elementary School was highly rated. We were ready to go. We bought a grand new TV. The first thing we watched showed Richard Nixon leaving Washington.

Cities Service and Tulsa have been good to us, bringing us growth, opportunities, adventures, and love beyond all expectations. When the moving van pulled in we started 39 golden years of true partnership which survives today after death did us part.

Easter at Grampy and Nanny Churchill's in New Jersey in about 1963. We spent many holidays there crossing the Hudson River from our home in Larchmont.

Phil and sons sailing in 1964. We chartered a large sailing yacht for a week and sailed to many parts around Long Island Sound.

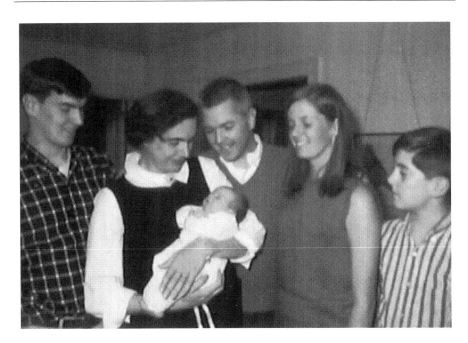

L to R, Art, Emily, Warren, Phil, Martha, Ben on Easter, April 10, 1966. Martha, 19, came home from Smith College to celebrate with her one week old brother, Warren. Phil and I were euphoric.

Six month old Warren was a joy. He never stopped smiling.

Larchmont 1967, L to R, Ben, Emily, Warren, Phil, Martha and Art.

Larchmont 1968. L to R, Art, Phil, Ben, Warren, Emily and Martha.

Ben nurtured his Bull Mastiff, Dolly, in his third floor
bedroom in Larchmont when she was not being walked or
penned. Warren loved her and pets her on our beloved
awninged patio.

Chapter 12. Tulsa 1974

Ages 49-56

Today, in the cool of the very early morning on August 13, 2015, in River Parks at a table on the bank of the Arkansas river, I enjoyed a cup of Quik Trip Coffee, sausage biscuit and The Tulsa World noting with sadness that ex-President Jimmy Carter had been diagnosed with cancer. A very large blue egret was sitting on a clump of branches arising from the full and flowing stream about thirty feet from shore. His long beak was visible as he turned his head to look around. I was filled with awe, wonder and a powerful visceral connection to my dear Phil and his respect for nature. The beauty of the scene brought my familiar tears of grief, gratitude, connection and appreciation.

As I looked down the river to the city, I remembered our move to Tulsa in 1974 with Cities Service forty-one years ago. Tulsa has been incredibly good to Phil and me. I love Tulsa. Phil loved Tulsa. Our horizons expanded beyond belief as our careers flourished, arts and education nourished us, politics engaged us, multiple global and multicultural interactions enriched us and All Souls Unitarian Church served as an immediate haven. Our house became the site of numerous family reunions, grandchildren's visits and sleep-overs, swimming parties, weekly Sunday night family dinners, and special holiday, anniversary and birthday celebrations. I hope that it was a place where our family found roots and wings as well as love.

Tulsa was a great place to raise Warren with the enrichment of Eliot Elementary, Carver Middle School, Booker T. Washington H.S., Philbrook Museum School, ice-skating rink downtown, public school orchestra, scouts, nearby lakes and streams for canoeing, zoo, etc., etc. Warren had excellent teachers, who were creative and project oriented in the Tulsa Public Schools. The mania for testing had not set in. Budget cuts were not the norm for education. There was no shortage of certified teachers. He experienced newly integrated schools to our joy. His outstanding scores on national tests proved that TPS had done its job. As a National Merit Scholar, he was well prepared for Oberlin College. Another bonus was that Phil was five minutes away from Warren's schools instead of the long commute. Phil effectively communicated with teachers and principals establishing a strong parental connection. Phil also was the

Cub Master and instigator of many Scout enrichment activities.

Our physical move from New York was a little unconventional. We arrived in a second hand gold Cadillac purchased for two hundred dollars from a neighbor for a fun, adventurous trip with many educational stops. It was mostly a fun trip except when we had radiator trouble and had to stop a few times. Warren invited his friend Mickey, the only African American in his second grade class, along for the trip. The boys had a blast, especially in motel pools until an ear infection finished that activity toward end of the trip. Tulsa neighbors welcomed us with lemonade as the expertly packed moving van pulled in and was unpacked, putting all furniture in pre-planned spaces in a house that had been meticulously renovated by the previous owners complete with shag carpet and lots of orange. It was the 1970s.

The physical move was easy. Our air conditioning and the many giant oaks on our green lot mitigated the one hundred degree August heat. Mickey flew back to New York. We were ready for work and school. Art, his new wife, Cathy, and daughter, Cynde, soon joined us, living a half a mile away so we had nearby Tulsa family. They were joined by baby Jason, for whom we kept a playpen and rocking chair. Jason, now in his late thirties, is a University of Tulsa engineering and computer grad and a manager at Level 3 in downtown Tulsa.

Phil was off to the impressive Cities Service building, now corporate headquarters, and just seven minutes from home. We gained two hours a day of family time without the New York commute to the historic former headquarters on Wall Street. Wonderful!! In New York, working for Cities for eight years, he had been vice-president of the Plastics and Special Projects Division, a job which he continued in Tulsa. In 1976, he became Vice President of Planning and Economics. The next quick rise was to Executive V.P. of Planning and Technology and ultimately Executive Vice President and Chief Financial Officer of Finance and Administration with many, many sectors reporting to him. His office (with a great bathroom) was between the CEO and the COO's. His office was so nice that Warren and I opted to spend many Saturdays there doing homework and lesson plans. I always felt that Cities was a very family friendly, spouse friendly company. The company culture nurtured us, and we thrived.

The perks, including company plane, were many and executive pay was good, but the ratio of the top compared to others had no resemblance to the obscene differences today. We did not buy big cars or a bigger house. In fact, Phil often drove a Moped to work during this period. Continuing to be a people person, he learned the name of everyone in the building so he could greet each by name in the elevator. Everyone loved Phil as usual, especially the night cleaner who made candles for him.

Phil had the ability to disagree with the status quo with a smile, and he advocated from his conscience. An example is that he resigned from the Petroleum Club when one of the female engineers reporting to him was refused entrance to the Men's Grille for a meeting (this was the 1970s and policy changed as a result). An advocate for women, he was selected Boss of Year by the Professional Secretaries Association, and he hired the first woman MBA from the University of Pennsylvania. He was especially good at team building with a loyal following of very enthusiastic supporters. All of this seemed ideal. We both reveled in the great social life that was spawned with me getting a wardrobe of the long dresses then in style. By night, I felt that I was a princess in Disneyland at company receptions and dinners whereas by day I was a growing teacher.

Cities also expected executives to give back to the community. Phil served on the boards of the Tulsa Opera, the Arts and Humanities as an officer, and the International Visitors, becoming its president, and the Girl Scouts, becoming vice-president. All of these organizations embraced his competence and extremely pleasing demeanor. All of these organizations opened up new experiences and vast enrichment for Phil, Warren and me.

For example, we took Warren to hear Pavarotti in San Diego on an opera trip. Cities Service supported my north side school with a playground. Many of my northside students rode in an elevator for the first time at the company building as Phil and I organized downtown field trips for them. I definitely was living a Tale of Two Cities - teaching on the north side by day and being an executive wife by night. It was the 1970s.

We were living in Camelot, but the economic forces of the day compelled Phil to disagree with other executives on some key decisions for saving the company from takeover, allocation of resources and building a new headquarters. Phil questioned whether he wanted to support actions with which he disagreed.

In deciding whether to retire or not, Phil and I had the most intense communication ever. We set up an easel in our kitchen and listed pros and cons. We used sticky notes. We went over budget and projections. We asked if he could walk away from an incredible job, even though his peers were men of integrity and goodwill. Phil would rather not support decisions which he could not embrace in regard to a new building and the acquisition/merger scene of the times. I concurred. We had communicated thoroughly about this major decision. Together, we had examined the facts and our feelings from every angle. We never, never regretted the decision made so thoughtfully together.

Phil resigned and was begged to stay, and he did for a year while training a replacement. He basically walked away from the golden parachutes so many others were getting as companies swallowed up other companies. However, he was happy with his decision, especially as he saw the layoffs as Cities was acquired by Occidental Petroleum after a long period of moves and countermoves by others who wanted Cities. Phil had been the one to answer the phone call from Boone Pickens when Boone Pickens had not yet become powerful.

Phil's retirement from Cities was marked by parties, drawings, and hundreds of leather bound letters. A wonderful era for us came to an end. When Phil returned home after his last day, he found his entire family from New York, Kansas and Tulsa at our house for a weekend of wishing him well. I had arranged a surprise for him. We presented him with a notebook of letters. Two of the letters follow. It was the early 1980s - the age of corporate takeovers.

Before his retirement from Cities Service as Chief Financial
Officer, Phil had many interesting experiences like being
lowered onto an oil rig in the Gulf of Mexico.

Art and his family lived in Tulsa. He designed and made many beautiful furniture pieces for us. This computer desk was innovative at the time.

Chapter 13. Letters from Warren and Ben to their dad as he retired from Cities Service Corporation

To Dad from Warren,

Here is a quote of Carlos Castaneda which begins **The Tao of Physics:** "Any path is only a path, and there is no affront, to oneself or to others, in dropping it if that is what your heart tells you . . . Look at every path closely and deliberate. Try it as many times as you think necessary. Then ask yourself, and yourself alone, one question . . . Does this path have a heart? If it does, the path is good; if it doesn't it is of no use."

It may be a presumptuous suggestion, but it seems to me that this quote has some bearing on what you are doing in retiring. Anyway, I congratulate you on dropping a path that you felt should no longer be followed. I wish you happiness on your future paths, and I feel sure that you will choose good ones.

Your choices are important to me. They affect my life, and I am glad that you're making, have made, this one. You have always been a helpful, kind, loving father to me and I will always be in your debt.

Congratulations.
Love,
Warren

To My Father from Ben,

My father always stays in my blood, whispering through my veins. I hear his voice from time to time. Sometimes when I need advice or I wonder what to do. Sometimes it's what I want to hear. But always I listen now. Sometimes I hear his voice for no reason that I know of. Sometimes I hear his voice in my voice when I speak to my son. Even though I don't see him so much, I get to know him better, now that I'm a father.

I know how much of himself he has given and gives to others. Much of what he has given, he has given just by being what he is. Never resigned, never without imagination, never without a sense of play, a project, a new skill or subject to delve into. Always solving problems or trying to instead of being complacent and adapting his behavior to suit the whim of the world or disorder.

I've never thanked him for the Saturday trips to museums, camping in the snow, touring the Civil War battlefields, snorkeling in Florida, building a proa. The proa: creature of imagination, creature of the weird, who else in the United States would build a 30" South Sea outrigger boat in their back yard. It lived a short life once it was formed. Only the sail and the ropes and the rigging survived. The pieces that caught the wind and gave the craft life. Some of the ropes have passed into the hands of the children. Ropes to pull our way through life. Ropes to tie our lives together. Ropes to lasso dreams. Rope, a simple thing - something basic, strong, adaptable. Much of what my father has given me is like a piece of rope.

My father has given much to his family and to the business world. He is now changing his relationship with the business world. He's becoming physically autonomous as well as mentally autonomous as he's always been. All those who have worked with him know they've worked with the best. But a man with a mind like my father's does not "retire". He does what he wants to do. He has accomplished the monumental task of putting himself in the position of endless possibility to his children. This has taken guts, strength, and love, year in and year out, and he is still young to boot. He is a slim survivor who is tender yet tough. I hope my children love me as much as his children love him.

Ben

For New Year's Eve 1981

Chapter 14, 1980s

1980 -1988 - 56 - 64 years old
Teaching, studying, exchanges and election

I am writing this on Saturday, August 15, 2015 at the Café
Cubana on Cherry Street, one of Phil's and my favorite
haunts, after buying tomatoes at the Farmers Market from
our favorite vendor. Today Phil was not behind me with his
usual supply of crisp bills or the waiting bag for the
produce, but he was with me in spirit as I walked past the
produce, the breads and plants. In the Café, I savor my
large strong black coffee and the delicious cranberry pecan
muffin which lift my spirits after a disturbing dream last
night in which I was barefoot walking down a long dusty
country road trying to get back to Phil.

Running into acquaintances and friends has always been a
farmers' market pleasure. Today two conversations
heartened me. One with an ex-city councilor who said Phil
and I had had a great run and the second with an ex-news

anchor who was grateful he could still walk and get around. Gratitude for a fantastic sixty-seven years replaced my grief. Positive vibes emanate from the market.

Today, I am recording memories of almost a decade of teaching, learning, teaming, exercising, loving, running for political office and communicating very effectively. We were a team. We were in the prime of life with a very successful thirty-four year corporate career ended and ready to enjoy new adventures to the max. The following decade was amazing. It was the 1980s. It was America.

Phil had long worked with the University of Kansas Business School in training programs for Cities personnel. This experience morphed into five retirement years of teaching as an Executive in Residence.

He modeled his weekly seminar after the case study method which he learned at the Harvard Business School and The Wharton School as an executive student. The Wall Street Journal was the text for the three hour weekly seminar supplemented by four hours of individual student interaction. I saw Professor Wood off on bus or by car in a tweed jacket with L.L. Bean Gore-Tex outerwear instead of the pinstripe suit. My heart still palpitated when he returned after a night away. I even presented a corporate wife history to his class. Mr. Chips was happy, relishing students, colleagues and teaching and so was Mrs. Chips who was teaching up a storm in the Tulsa Public Schools.

A huge family bonus was that Ben simultaneously studied at K.U. Law school (he later had a very distinguished career in leading public defense for the state of Kansas). Maggie got her Masters in Social Work at K.U. We (and especially) Phil had many wonderful interactions observing nature and art with our precious grandchildren, Nick and Celeste, at the museums, walking around the beautiful K.U. campus or along the river, eating at the very interesting ethnic restaurants along the interesting main street of Lawrence.

Son Art sold his Tulsa woodworking business to a company in Hutchinson, Kansas and moved his family of wife Kathy and children Cynde, Jason, and Jon there. We had family reunions with the two Kansas families in the then very popular Holidomes (it was the 1980s). On our most memorable Holidome New Year's Eve extravaganza, Martha and grandson Sam came from New Jersey to help us welcome baby Virginia Ruth, Art and Cathy's fourth child. Phil and I packed the car with crockpots and coolers to produce an in room feast. Older children reveled in hot tubs, a pool, slides, horns, and throwing rolls of paper over balconies. Kansas Holidomes were a frequent Wood meeting site.

Back home in Tulsa, Phil and I were the founding co-chairs

of a Booker T. Washington American Foreign Service exchange program with frequent meetings at our house establishing rules, support and schedules for a thriving multi-country foreign exchange. Fabricio Barriga from Ecuador lived with us for a year as our "son" and Warren's brother. We drove him for haircuts, dates, tutored him in American history, read English novels with him, and took him camping in New Mexico. Phil, Warren and I later visited him in Ecuador marveling at the barefoot maid wearing a hat as she washed our dishes. We also marveled at the Andes and architecture. We still correspond.

Phil and I were chaperones for Warren's Japanese language class on a three week exchange trip to Japan. We had a Japanese homestay in Utsunomiya, sleeping on Tatami mats, bathing in a communal bath and kneeling on the floor to eat raw fish with chopsticks. We loved our host family. Out of this trip, I created a culture box which became the prototype for a whole 40 country collection housed at Eisenhower International School today in the Emily Wood Room. Phil gave his Japanese slideshow at numerous schools, churches and civic programs. He balanced his checkbook using an abacus. Utsunomiya later became a Tulsa Sister City.

Phil became president the International Visitors of Tulsa, an affiliate of the Washington, D.C. office. The U.S. Department of State sent a steady stream of visitors to

Tulsa. Warren, a foreign language maven, encouraged us to entertain many in our home, which we did with gusto. A highlight of Phil's presidency was a very comprehensive China conference. I co-authored a large China book for teachers.

After a five year K.U. experience, Phil decided to study for the prestigious Chartered Financial Analyst exam to help him manage his retirement money. He did most of his study at home with a few review sessions in bigger cities and an exam in Los Angeles. He finished in the top three percent worldwide. He simultaneously had a part time job with Rubottom Dudash, financial advisors.

I, meanwhile, was experiencing great professional growth in teaching Social Studies and Gifted Education in the Tulsa Public Schools. Phil was a partner in many innovative projects involving economics, Japan, law, and art, for which I was the recipient of several state awards. In 1988, Phil was surprised by a visit from a prestigious city leader who asked him to run as a Democrat for the Tulsa City Commission. Our life changed completely when after much communication with me, he said yes. He ran for Tulsa City Auditor.

We enjoyed a political fervor as we raised money and campaigned. I got very good at installing union made signs in yards. Phil handled all of the paper work meticulously with great attention to detail and he spoke at numerous forums and coffees. Politics was in my blood since my father and other forbearers had been Mayor of our New Jersey Township. A mailing piece was produced and Phil did a radio ad. We campaigned very hard using our corporate connections and my north and south side school connections. Phil had a formidable opponent who had experience in city government and who had a tremendous will to win. Phil won by a very small margin. Twenty-one wonderful years as Tulsa city Auditor began in April, 1988.

It was a fantastic April week for the Wood family. Phil was elected. I was named Tulsa Teacher of the Year (Oklahoma semi- finalist). Son Warren, Oberlin Senior, won a scholarship and teaching assistantship at Penn State. We were starting again on a great new adventure at age sixty-four. We seemed to thrive on adventure, change, learning, excitement, new goals and communication.

BEN (CHIEF APELLATE DEFENDER)
MAGGIE + NICK + CELESTE

WARREN (OBERLIN JUNIOR)

GREETINGS!
FROM
PHIL + EMILY WOOD

ART (ARCHITECTURAL MILLWORK)
KATHY + JASON + JONATHAN + CYNDE

MARY (ARCHITECT) + SAM

DECEMBER 1985

Christmas greeting. Our family was scattered, but we gathered often.

Clockwise starting at 1, Sam, Martha, Art, Jason, Jon, Cathy, Cynde, Emily, Warren, Phil, Ben, Nick and Celeste. Taken at a Thanksgiving gathering.

In 1982 we chaperoned Warren's Booker T. Washington
High School Japanese class to Japan. Here Phil lays
groundwork for future Sister City relationship with
Utsunomiya City Councilors.

Chapter 15. Letter from Phil and poem on the occasion of Emily's 75th birthday - 2000

Prologue

Last night I leaned forward and said softly to you, "Dear, there is something that I must ask you. It has always bothered me that our fourth child never quite looked like the rest of our children.

Now I want to assure you that these 53 years have been the most wonderful experience I could have ever hoped for, and your answer cannot take that all away. But, I must know, did he have a different father?

You dropped your head, unable to look me in the eye, you paused for moment and then confessed. "Yes, yes he did." I was very shaken, the reality of what you admitted hit me harder than I had expected. With a tear in my eye I asked, "Who? Who was he? Who was the father?" Again you dropped your head, saying nothing at first as you tried to muster the courage to tell me the truth. Then, finally, you said, "You."

Thanks to you I am not the same man I was. In thinking about what you have done for/with me I thought your resume might help me organize some words about what your life means to me. Webster's New Collegiate Dictionary says a resume is "a short account of one's career and qualifications prepared typically by an applicant for a position. If I just printed yours out. It is seven pages long! How, then, am I to dignify seventy-five years in a page or two? I don't even know how to the compress the three score years we have known each other. There may be inaccuracies in my following memories but I know you will forgive me as you always do.

As my father said when he learned we were engaged, "thank God! - a person of strong character may save him." Being head of the Honor Board at Smith College backed up your record as a live-in student proctor at Kent Place School. Both positions gave you excellent experience in dealing with wayward youth. Thank you for the heroic job you did in helping me keep my eye on the ball. Hormones were kept in check by the lake in winter in Northampton during Charity Ball in 1942. Again the hormones were tamed in the tobacco fields of the Connecticut River valley on furlough in 1944. You sure made June 22, 1946 a BIG day.

There have been times when we have been apart. World War II was an example. You were working on Vegacre Farm harvesting broccoli while I was in the 10th Mountain Division. Letters were so important and you were and are so good at writing them - making me feel close to you. The telephone was not the convenient bargain then that it is now.

I appreciate the unbelievable sacrifices you have made on my account. You graduated cum laude from Smith a few days before our marriage. After a bucolic honeymoon in the Adirondacks you were stuck in Brown Hall dormitory on the fourth floor in an apartment with no bath and no running water! How you cooked pies and chicken croquettes on a one burner hotplate I'll never know. Remember when the grocer asked if we were having company when you ordered three slices of baloney instead of the usual two? Not only were living conditions rudimentary, but also Princeton would not even allow you to peek into a classroom. We moved twice that year with no car. Even so, our dates going out to dinner on our bicycles were a great treat. I have fond memories of dinners at Lahierre's and the diner on route 29. As always, you were proactive and got a job teaching at Miss Fine's School. You rode your bicycle a couple of miles to work every day even though you were pregnant with Martha. Her birth during the 1947 reunion was the beginning of another era. I wept at her beauty at birth.

Before moving to St. Louis we moved at least two more times to Pop Pop's and Mrs. Drake's homes. I bought our house in St. Louis without your ever having seen it! You arrived by train with Martha, moved in and the next day I left with our only car (a company car) on a two-week trip to Texas. When I arrived back you had bought Polly the Scotty (aka Polyitis Nooney), made fast friends with the neighbors, the Deans, the Hinrichs and the MacGregors. You walked to the trolley (or was it a bus - I never had to do it so I don't remember too well) to go to the grocery store. You trained Martha to send me off on business trips each week saying 'get dat order'. I well remember the call to me in Indianapolis at RCA when you took a cab to St. Luke's maternity ward in downtown St. Louis. I set a record and arrived just in time for big Art's birth. We stayed together for a couple of hours and I went home. A short time later a nurse called saying you had a baby boy, everyone was fine and there was no need for me to come to the hospital (in those days they really knocked you out so you did not remember my visit!) How about the move back to New Jersey in 1953! You handled it alone with Martha, Arthur and Polly traveling by train even after taking Arthur to have his stomach pumped because he may have swallowed turpentine! By then Mart had already been in schools in Missouri and New Jersey. You always helped the transitions by inviting the teachers for dinner.

Late 1953 saw us moving to Benton Harbor where again you quickly established friendships and support systems with Dr. Blanning, the Boermas, Howards, Shaws, Clarks, Byrns, Insleys, and Parretts. Except for Rev. Blanning, we still keep in touch with all of them through your efforts. You really needed a support system since I traveled out of town five days a week. We also moved once during the three and a half years in Benton Harbor. Ben was born and you were elected to the Alumni Council of Smith College at the age of 29. I have warmhearted memories the loving receptions you gave me when I returned home each Friday night and how the children were primed to treat me like royalty.

You made the move to Northfield for my Chicago job a growth experience. Could that be forty-four years ago? You kindly helped me remember the important things in life such as love, family, health and perspective as I became a 'big shot'. As usual, you found old friends, made new friends and established connections quickly. You prescribed dancing lessons that brought us closer together and give us pleasure to this day.

Two score years ago we made our 'last move' to Larchmont and headquarters of Union Carbide. By now, we decided that raising Mart, Art and Ben was so much fun that we should have Warren after a lapse of twelve years from Ben's birth. With fondness and humor I remember the reaction of our three when you announced his forthcoming birth at dinner at the Washington Arms in Mamaroneck. You keep fresh in my mind so many good memories of Larchmont; Warren's natural birth, great dinner parties at home, friends we still communicate with (for example - Anderson, Clausen, Dhramsey, Evans, Frank, Holden, Hopf, Johnson, Kanter, Keller, Pugh, Reynolds, Shyer, Sleeper, Sloane, Smith, Sterbenz, Tebbens and Young), getting an MAT at Manhattanville, starting teaching again, boating, ice skating, camping on Key Largo in a storm, driving Volkswagens on the cross Bronx expressway, meeting at the World's Fair after work, cub scouts, mariner girl scouts, editing the Junior League magazine, and much more. In view of all that, can you believe I thank you from the bottom of my heart for convincing me to move to Tulsa? You know how to keep your/my eye on the ball.

The walls around the computer I am using say a lot about the Tulsa experience. About forty plaques (Oklahoma Medal for excellence in Teaching, National Council for the Social Studies Elementary Teacher of the Year, Oklahoma Education Association Instructional Excellence Award, Oklahoma Bar Association Liberty Bell Award, Oklahoma

Supreme Court Teacher of the Year, American Lawyers Auxiliary LRE Elementary Teacher of the Year, Oklahoma Council for the Social Studies Teacher of the Year), pictures (with Senator Boren and President Bush, Governor Bellmon, head of the Oklahoma Bar Association, climbing Mt. Summit in Colorado, attending my inauguration dance), proclamations (Tulsa Public Schools Teacher of the Year, The Warren E. Burger National Repository for Educational Materials on Citizenship and the Constitution for creative teaching materials, Jewish Educator's Council Certificate of Service) and more surround me. Another testimony to your contributions is the fact that there is no place in Tulsa we can go without a former student coming up and talking with you in admiration and respect for the teaching you have done.

I revel in the beautiful excitement of living with you. You show me how to make work almost magically evaporate into enjoyment. Some current evidence is that as President of Smith '46, President of the UN Association of Eastern Oklahoma, board of directors of the National Council for the Social Studies, board directors of the Tulsa Global Alliance, teacher at Tulsa Community College and teacher at Heritage Academy you still have time for mothering, grand mothering, cooking, shopping for groceries, swimming, taking daily walks together, travel, making love, reading the paper in bed, washing my clothes and keeping up with friends both past and present. Thank you and I love you.

[signature]

April 11, 2000

Epilogue

A favorite sonnet by Shakespeare sums up some of my feelings for you.

When in disgrace with fortune and men's eyes
I all alone beweep my outcast state,
And trouble deaf heaven with my bootless cries,
And look upon myself, and curse my fate;

Wishing me like to one more rich in hope,
Featur'd like him, like him with friends possess'd,
Desiring this man's art, and that man's scope,
With what I most enjoy contented least;

Yet in these thoughts myself almost despising,
Haply I think on Thee-and then my state,
Like to the lark at break of day arising
From sullen earth, sings hymns at heaven's gate;

For thy sweet love remember'd, such wealth brings That
then I scorn to change my state with kings.

The family gathered in 1990 to watch Emily receive the
Oklahoma Medal in Elementary Teaching presented by
President George Bush. L to R back, Emily, Martha, Ben,
then Senator David Boren, Warren, Auditor Phil. Front L to
R, Celeste, Nick and Sam.

Phil took this picture of me at the Oklahoma Foundation for Excellence receiving an award in 1990. L to R, Speaker of the House, Carl Albert, President George H. W. Bush, Senator Don Nichols, Senator David Boren at podium.

On vacation in 1991, celebrating our 45th wedding
anniversary with a one week rafting trip through the Grand
Canyon where we camped at night. It was a great adventure
sponsored by the Princeton Geology Dept.

Grand Canyon adventure with Princeton Alumni 1991.
When not riding the raft the length of the canyon, we
played in the water.

We celebrated our 50th wedding anniversary in 1996, at age 71. Shown here in robes from Lebanon, a gift from Abir's parents.

This was taken at a large luncheon in the Vista Room of the Gilcrease Museum with family and friends from across the country at our 50th anniversary.

Early exchange to San Luis Potosi, Mexico. Emily started an exchange with Instituto Cervantes, a private school in Tulsa's Mexican Sister City and the new Eisenhower International School where she was lead teacher. The exchange lasted about twenty years until drug violence stopped it. Here she is shown with left, Anna Judd, Mexican First Coordinator and Ilanke Restovic, Second Mexican coordinator and Phil at a picnic in SLP. Phil often chaperoned in transit and visited Mexican elected officials.

2010 - Zane, Emily and Phil with Zane's host family arriving at airport. We were chaperones and coordinators for this 19th Eisenhower Exchange, three years before Phil died and nineteen years after Emily had started it.

Phil and Emily also traveled to Amiens, France many times to coordinate and chaperone an Eisenhower Exhchange.

Chapter 16. Progeny

I am filled with gratitude as I recollect so many happy times as our progeny expanded with the addition of nine grandchildren and six great grandchildren, plus two step grandchildren. Their family love, caring, wit, and wisdom blessed Phil and me with lots of fun and joy. We were distressed by some of their bad fortunes, but we strove to succor in times of loss and sickness. We tried. All children, in turn, were always there for us to share our pleasure. For example, a month before Phil died, we savored food, art, and gardens at the Philbrook Art Museum, a movie, an elegant brunch at the Polo Grill and a home dinner. It was an ideal last weekend before a three week hospital stint. A month later children and grandchildren sat at his Memorial Service remembering as we listened to the soulful rendition of the song, "What a Wonderful World." Tears welled when "I Can't Stop Loving You" was sung. Mayor Susan Savage and son Ben gave moving eulogies.

We experienced the delight of having nine grandchildren grow from cuddly infants to engaging toddlers. We visited their schools, games, art shows and scout troops. We even were chaperones on an exchange trip to Mexico with Zane. Currently, in 2015, their educational status includes a PhD (Jon), seven Bachelor's degrees, a college freshman and a high school junior. Celeste is enrolled in a Master of Fine Arts program and Virginia is taking graduate education courses. We were grateful that all who were old enough are college graduates. Education mattered to us. We reveled in graduations, too numerous to mention. One example was Jason's Oklahoma School of Science and Math on the Oklahoma Capitol steps.

As children, some grandchildren lived or live in Tulsa. Some did not, but visited for holidays and during summer vacations. However, all swam in our pool, joined in family dinners around our dining room table and visited the zoo and museums with us. Most attended Nutcracker Ballet as a family tradition. Nick's passionate boyhood interest in fountains led us on a discovery of Tulsa's water jets. Papa Phil cooked many a waffle during Sami and Zane's sleepovers.

We also traveled to our see our grandchildren many times. Here are but a very few examples. We went to Hutchinson, Kansas to see high schooler Cynde model for Dillard's with poise and aplomb. We savored our trips to Baltimore and Princeton to cheer for Sam, Syracuse Lacrosse star, while savoring the excellent tailgate food and drink prepared by Ron and Martha. Our trip to meet eight month old Sami, born in the United Arab Emirates, was our most exotic. We were bumped from our British Airways flight to the unbelievably luxurious Emirates Airline for the experience of a lifetime. Landing in and visiting incredible opulent Dubai were preludes to visiting Warren and Abir's very spacious apartment provided by the university where Warren taught math. We checked in on Sami's progress two years later when he was summering with his Farhat grandparents in beautiful, beautiful Beirut on the Mediterranean. Zane was a bump in Abir's stomach at that time.

Trips with Virginia to Disneyland, Little Rock, and Kansas and many museums were precious times with her.

Big event celebrations brought us together many times. All of our progeny, siblings, and in-laws were at Martha and Ron's stellar firehouse wedding in New Jersey dancing up a storm. Martha subsequently went on to design an extensive rescue building incorporating the fire department, as well as water rescue boats. A room in the building is named after her. Another festive wedding reception was Art and Patricia's at the Petroleum Club of Tulsa, again with lots of family and dancing. Many of us gathered for the beautiful wedding of Jon and Ellen in Norman, Oklahoma. At the peacock themed barn wedding of grandson Nick and Erika near Ithaca, New York. Phil, at 85 years, got down and dirty on his haunches and did his famous Russian dance to the delight of children and grandchildren.

Notable was our 50th wedding anniversary at the zoo in 1996 with a pasta dinner at the elephant house and huge luncheon at the Gilcrease Museum. Environmentalist granddaughter Celeste was ahead of the rest of us in questioning the practice of keeping elephants in captivity in zoos. I am proud of the thoughtfulness of our grandchildren. They are passionate about their beliefs, which encompass a wide spectrum politically and religiously. Phil and I welcomed this huge diversity of thought among our family. We looked back and contemplated our love of discussion of multiple ideas. Sami was the youngest grandchild in attendance at our 50th, having been just born in the United Arab Emirates three months before. Mother Ruth did not make it to Tulsa, but many of us were at her 100th birthday two months later for another family roundup.

Another large scale celebration was on Phil's 80th birthday at the Doubletree in 2004 featuring dancing. Dancing up a storm were grandchildren Sam, Cynde and her husband Rick, Jason, Jon and Ellen, Cathy, Amy, Sami and Zane.

Martha and Ron gave a follow up in New York for the 80th for those who could not make it to Tulsa.

Phil's and my last big dance in was at Hispanic Foundation's 2012 Noche de Gala with daughter Martha, my sister Martha, niece Pace, son Warren, and grandsons Sami and Zane. We were marking twenty years of galas, awards, feasting and dancing.

All was not dancing and fun for our children. They experienced some very hard times. Phil and I always agreed that we would be there for our progeny whether the problem was health, divorce or death. We discussed and agreed on many methods to help. Once in agreement we executed our decisions. Our underlying philosophy was to "do what we can." After we had done "what we could," we accepted our limitations using meditation and conversation over a drink to find peace. We always reached a mutual agreement. We were on the same page.

Our children present us with a beautiful pillow on the occasion of our 50th documenting our wonderful life. L to R, Emily, Warren, Phil in 1996.

2008 - Phil's 84th birthday with four generations including great grandchildren Jackson, Alex and Mitch. Beautiful Patricia, daughter-in-law with hand on Art's shoulder died of cancer after this.

Chapter 17. Auditor

1988 - 2009 Ages 64 – 85

On August 31, 2015, my heart swelled with pride and love, when the Philip W. Wood Atrium at Tulsa City Hall was dedicated in a moving ceremony remembering his twenty-one years of service as Tulsa City Auditor. Phil Wood was Tulsa's longest serving elected official. First elected City Auditor at age 64, he won 11 elections until defeat at age 85 in a Republican sweep of state and local elections. Asked by Democrats to run in 1988, victory was greatly helped by the Local Teamsters production of hundreds of blue and white yard signs, which were deposited in huge piles in our family room making the race totally real to us as we plotted the implantation of signs in hundreds of yards.

He was proud to run as a Democrat with union support. I first joined the teachers OEA and NEA as I taught in inner city schools. In 1978, Phil was an executive vice-president of Cities Service where most of his colleagues were

Republicans. He supported me 100% citing the fact that many of his perks were the result of union demands for social security, health insurance, and fair work hours and pay. I know I always felt better knowing I had a safety net to protect me in case of playground accidents, etc.. We put up hundreds of signs together getting to know the byways and highways. Auditing was completely nonpolitical and nonpartisan. Running for office was political as we fought a very hard campaign against an extremely determined Republican who raised enough money for a series of very dramatic TV ads. Phil won with a very, very slender margin. As an auditor, his work was independent, fair, and completely nonpartisan.

Election Day in April 1988 was a red-letter day. Phil won. I was chosen Tulsa Teacher of the Year (Oklahoma semifinalist). Warren received a fully funded – salaried fellowship for graduate Math study and teaching at Pennsylvania State University. The Tulsa World Editorial page congratulated the three of us. Celebration continued that spring as Warren graduated from Oberlin and granddaughter Cynde from Hutchinson Junior College before going on to get her B.S. from Emporia State.

When Phil was elected in 1988, Tulsa had a commission form of government with the mayor and auditor a member of the commission. All were elected at large which resulted in a commission greatly skewed toward whites living in a midtown prosperous district. In 1988, a new charter was adopted with 9 geographic council districts each electing their own representative. Thus, a more democratic form of government was born. Phil was the last auditor under the commission form of government and the first under the council form of government. The new charter brought new minority faces to the council and it was a fresh day even though Mayor Randle and Auditor Wood continued.

Mayor Randle served as an excellent Master of Ceremonies at the 2015 dedication introducing an historic spectrum of people who had worked with Phil for the 21 years of 1988-2009. Mayor Randle blended humor, respect and nostalgia. I was very happy that he called me Phil's true partner. When I was asked to speak, I was delighted but afraid that I would get too emotional. I decided to pretend that I was giving a campaign speech as I had when we campaigned. Phil ran 12 times with 11 victories. I had many roles in my 71 years of adoring him. I relished roles of campaigner and auditor's wife.

I was delighted that our daughter Martha and husband Ron came from N.J. joining son Arthur and son Warren to remember their Dad. Grandson Jason, had a short elevator ride from his Level 3 job. He was with his girlfriend Amy. Grandson Sami, University of Tulsa freshman, and Zane, Booker T.Washington Junior, remembered their beloved Papa.

Many thanks to the many people who made this dream a reality - especially Auditor Cathy Criswell who persisted through meeting after meeting. The council resolution was key, with my Councilor GT Bynum a special help, as was the continued support of Dwain Midget of the Mayor's office. The Arts Commission was instrumental in the design of the stunning installation which harmonizes so beautifully with the room. Two of Phil's longtime friends and fellow 1970s board members from the Arts and Humanities Joan Seay and Linda Frazier were vital in making sure of the compatibility of the plaque with the architecture of City Hall. Mayor Susan Savage spoke eloquently.

Phil had supported charter change wholeheartedly after realizing first hand as I taught at Alcott, Whitman and Gilcrease that Tulsa was indeed a tale of two cities. The northside was not represented at all. After charter change, he truly liked working with the inspirational councilors B.S. Roberts and Dorothy Dewitty.

He took his job - the responsibilities of being auditor – seriously, but he never took himself seriously. Repeat, he took the job of being Tulsa City Auditor very, very seriously but he did not take himself seriously - he always kept perspective and a sense of humor.

There are so many things he loved about being auditor that I can't name them all.

First of all, he enjoyed his team of city auditors - Ron Maxwell was his rock and right hand man. The audit department was a second family.

He loved making the auditor a viable, independent, strong third part of the city government by using cooperation rather than confrontation.

He loved the chance to use technology to do huge independent projects like codifying all the ordinances for the first time much to the delight of the legal department. He copyrighted a Bird Dog search engine for retrieving relevant city information.

He loved serving in the professional AIA at national, state and local levels to bring spectacular excellence and national recognition to the department.

He loved learning. He became a Certified Internal Auditor after three years of study. Studying to become a Certified Fraud Examiner was another challenge which he embraced.

He loved serving on the Tulsa Housing Authority Audit Committee and analyzing the complexity of federal grants as well as other revenue sources.

He loved visiting and representing Tulsa at six Sister Cities (San Luis Potosi, Celle, Amiens, Utsunomiya, Tiberias, and Zelenograd). I always went. We made many friends. We hosted scores of international visitors at work and at home.

He loved helping educate children about government facilitating many student interactive visits at City Hall. He was proud of the Police and Fire Departments and tried to attend all graduations. He served on the OK State Police Pension board with pride. He was committed to every audit whether it was of heavy equipment like the Hazmat truck or a gun in the property room.

He loved working at TU with students who were studying auditing. He enjoyed sitting on the OU Business School Board of Governors.

He loved the Arts and being season subscribers to ballet, Chamber Music Tulsa, opera and symphony.

He always was very interested in facilities and city employees working at the Performing Arts Center.

After a wonderful performance at the PAC, we would stand look back at the sky line. I would always say, "Your City is looking good." He would always smile. It was a good moment repeated after every performance. Remembering the moment brings tears to my eyes but gratitude for the Arts in Tulsa. Experiencing the music of the Tulsa Symphony and Chamber Music Tulsa alone since his death is an emotional and spiritual experience for me.

We always held hands. It was magic. I can't do that now, but he is there through the beauty of the music and the dancers.

The first swearing in after charter change in 1990. Phil
stands next to Mrs. Judy Randle who stands next to her
husband, Mayor Roger Randle on the steps of old City Hall.
The newly elected first council is on the left.

Swearing in at the Gilcrease Museum when Kathy Taylor was Mayor. L to R, Abir, Warren, Art, Emily, Phil, Martha Wood and Judge Jane Wiseman. Judge Wiseman, a respected friend, swore him in 10 times.

Phil represented Tulsa at several Sister Cities while he was Auditor. Here he is with the Mayor of Zelengrad, Russia. Our delegation delivered medical supplies. Phil and I later hosted Dr. Zonka from Zelengrad in Tulsa.

Entertaining international visitors at home in 1992. Phil also entertained many international visitors at City Hall. I was proud to show off Eisenhower International School to numerous delegations.

Trip to Israel Sister City Tiberias, dancing on the Sea of
Galilee in 1995. We loved our dance! Auditor Wood had
many meetings with auditors there.

We accompanied Mayor Susan Savage on a 1995 visit to Israel and Tiberias. Emily visited many schools. Phil had many government meetings, but at night, we danced on a dinner boat on the Sea of Galilee.

Israel Sister Cities trip. Phil in Bethlehem being sold a headdress.

At Martin Luther King, Jr. Day Parade. L to R, Virginia Wood, Phil, Emily, Dr. Zonka from Russia.

Global Vision Award from Tulsa Global Alliance was presented by Mayor Bill LaFortune. I also treasure a solar globe from the United Nations with the inscription, "Thank you to a remarkable man."

Grandchildren Zane and Sami accompany us to Hispanic American Foundation Noche de Gala when Papa won the Award of the Americas. They later went when I received it.

Auditor Phil always spent time at the Democratic Party booth at the Tulsa State Fair. Here he is with grandsons, Zane and Sami. Being elected every two years was political. Serving as Auditor was strictly non-political for Phil.

I stop often at this sign at 15ᵗʰ and Lewis entrance to the expressway. I sit and sip a Braum's latte in the parking lot. I am happy that hundreds of drivers see this. 2010 photo.

On September 1, 2015, the Atrium at Tulsa City Hall was dedicated to the memory of Auditor Phil Wood, longest serving Tulsa elected official. Family attending L to R, Zane Wood, Ron Subber, Art Wood, Sami Wood, Amy Gerald, Warren Wood, Jason Wood, Martha Wood Subber and Emily. The Arts Commission was active in designing the plaque. Present Auditor Cathy Criswell worked tirelessly for the project. Former Mayor Roger Randle was a brilliant Master of Ceremonies introducing a host of dignitaries.

Chapter 18. Finale

The Unknown Expanse

I'VE LOST MYSELF,
SOMEWHERE IN THE DISTANCE
BEYOND THE EYE'S REACH;
I RESIDE IN THE LANDS I CANNOT SEE.

THERE IS A PROMISE
IN THE LIMITS OF THE HORIZON
OF THE CONTINUING STRETCH
OF THE EARTH,
SO THAT AS I FACE
THE SCENE OF CONTEMPLATION,
IT IS THE UNSEEABLE
MY EYES FIX ON.

~Celeste Wood

Poem by my beloved daughter and my father's beloved granddaughter selected by my beloved mother for Dad's memorial service program last month. Celeste's poetry touched both of her grandfathers deeply. – Ben Wood

Phil Wood died two years ago. Our love did not die. A Day of the Dead (Dias del Muertes) simulation ceremony was borrowed from the Mexican Catholic tradition at All Souls Unitarian Church. As I placed his picture and a paper flower on the colorful altar, I felt love and joy. A peaceful acceptance of death as a part of life swept over me. The candles, flowers, paper cut outs, skeletons, skulls and numerous pictures of the dead on the ofrenda with music and costumed dance celebrated love. I returned home to Methodist Manor, reminded of our Protestant heritage, and made my own ofrenda with his pictures, paper flowers and Mexican souvenirs. The Central American Catholic based tradition brought love and joy. Acceptance of death as universal also came as I called out his name in the Jewish tradition during the service.

My story has been about the importance of communication in our love affair. Immediately after his death, I communicated by writing him notes on nice stationery and putting them in his sock drawer. Then I bought a fine leather journal and wrote to him every day for nine months. Tears flowed as I told him my activities and thoughts of each day. I went to school, church, meetings, concerts and events. I told him all. Love and communication were still alive.

I also wanted to share my love for him with the world. I contributed toward a plaque on a bench in the beautiful Linnaeus Garden in loving memory of Auditor Phil Wood. I sit on the bench in front of the crystal clear pool with its fountain splashing over rugged Oklahoma basalt pillars. I see holly, rose of sharon, roses, and begonias offering their pollen to bees and butterflies. Our love lives on.

Underwriting a Chamber Music Concert in Phil's memory on my 90th birthday brought our love to family and friends as we savored the joyous Modigliani Quartet. It was a transformational moment of sharing incredible music.

Encouraging the creation of the beautiful Philip Warren Wood auditorium with its magnificent plaque and smiling picture reflects the love he felt for his job as Auditor and the City of Tulsa. He is described as a genial man on the plaque.

Love lives on in Phil's children and grandchildren, who in turn are loving people.

Phil is dead, but our love that started on a moonlit night under the Graduate Tower in Princeton in 1941, 74 years ago, burns bright. It was fabulous. It is still magic. I am blessed.

Peace, salaam, shalom to all.

Phil, in his mid-eighties dancing down and dirty at Nick and Erica's wedding three years before he died to the delight of his children and grandchildren. He always wanted to do the Russian dance. I sometimes restrained him.

We danced until near the end. Probably, we were counting out the waltz.

Garden Gate in Nyack, NY by Ben, 2012. Our last travel.

Bench dedicated to City Auditor Phil Wood in the Linnaeus Teaching Garden in Woodward Park, Tulsa. I take my lunch and sit on this bench frequently by the fountain. Tears of remembrance flow. I also am moved by the orange and black carp in the pool when I visit the garden. Phil is with me.

Family Pictures

I have reveled in looking at some of our family pictures. I have given many to my children, so many have already been passed on. What follows is a sampling which does not do justice to the many wonderful times we shared on holidays, trips, meals, graduations, visits, celebrations, etc. etc.

I ask forgiveness and understanding for any omissions. Advanced age and lack of technical skills are my excuses. I feel gratitude and love for my progeny as I look at the images which follow. They were part of the magic.

Emily and Phil with attendants at Martha and Ron's wedding at the Firehouse in Clinton, NJ (a huge family gathering). L to R, Celeste Wood, Virginia Wood, Amy Subber, Cathy Subber, Sam Bassett.

Martha and Ron's wedding. L to R, Bride Martha, Sam Bassett, Ron Subber, Emily and Phil.

Sam playing Lacrosse for Syracuse at Princeton. L to R, Martha, Sam, Emily, Nick.

Sam Bassett was a Captain of the Syracuse Lacrosse Team which won the 2000 NCAA Division I Championship at Byrd Stadium at the University of Maryland. They defeated Princeton in the finals for the championship.

There were five captains, so Sam was a captain, not *the* captain. It was a huge honor for him because he was a transfer student from Herkimer County Community College his Junior year.

Art's family. L to R, Jon, Jason, Ginnie, Cynde Wood.

Petroleum Club Santa. L to R, Jon, Emily, Phil with
Virginia on Santa's lap.

Papa loved receiving this from Jason. We treasured
grandchildren made cards and pictures.

1988. This was the first college graduation of a grandchild which we attended - Many more followed. This shows Cynde graduating from Junior College in Hutchinson, Kansas. She later got her B.A. from Emporia State. We got up at three o'clock the next morning to be back for Phil's new City Auditor job and my teaching job as New Tulsa Teacher of the year.

Patricia and Art at Phil's 80th birthday. Our entire family and many friends from across the country attended our 80th birthday and 59th wedding anniversary party at the Doubletree Hotel in December, 2004. All ages danced to a great band.

Nick and Celeste Wood, as we saw them in Lawrence, KS.

June 3, 1991 - At Emporia State University when Nick was
recognized by Duke University – Phil, Nick, Ben, Warren

June 3, 1991 – At Emporia State University when Nick was recognized by Duke University – Emily, Celeste, and her mother, Maggie.

Nick's engagement picture with Erika. When they married in a barn near Ithaca New York, a lot of family joyfully gathered.

The Wood males at Nick's wedding. L to R, Jason, bridegroom Nick, Ben, Warren, Zane, Phil and Sam Bassett.

Abir, Sami, Warren and Zane in 1999. We enjoyed having them live at our house after they returned from several years living in the United Arab Emirates where both boys were born and Warren taught. Phil and I found our two trips to the Emirates to be great adventures. For example, as we drove across the desert, a reclining camel blocked our way for a long time. Camel races in opulent Dubai were new.

Papa Phil made waffles for Sami and Zane after sleepovers. Papa liked flowers on the table.

The beautiful Coulson family of Cynde, Alex, Mitch and Rick. Alex and Mitch are our oldest great Grandchildren.

Beautiful family of Jon and Ellen Wood. L to R, Jackson, Ellen, Parker, Jon, Lincoln and Olivia. Parker and Lincoln were born after Phil died, but he loved holding Jackson and Olivia.

L to R, Emily, Phil, Jon, Ellen Wood at wedding in Norman, OK in 2005.

Great-grandfather Phil with Olivia not too long before he died.

We enjoyed a trip to Branson with our family. Shown here at the Titanic Museum are back row, Warren, Art, Emily, Phil. Middle row, Abir, Patricia, Sami. Front row, Zane.